It's Your Life
Take Authority

It's Your Life
Take Authority

A Spiritual Guide For Your Life

Angela Hood

authorHOUSE®

AuthorHouse™
1663 Liberty Drive
Bloomington, IN 47403
www.authorhouse.com
Phone: 1-800-839-8640

First published by AuthorHouse   9/2/2009

ISBN: 978-1-4389-8616-6 (sc)

Library of Congress Control Number: 2009909021

Printed in the United States of America
Bloomington, Indiana

This book is printed on acid-free paper.

Table of Contents

Acknowledgements

Truly, this book would not be possible without the support of my lovely husband Bishop Hood. Thank you for your prayers and words of encouragement. I am blessed to be married to a wonderful man like yourself.

To my children Elijah and Angelica, thank you for understanding and putting up with mom's busy schedule.

To New Life my church family thanks for your prayers and support

To my amazing sister Tonita McEntyre thank you for pushing me to continue even when I wanted to give up.

Pastor Joyce God sent you into my life at the right time, your words of encouragement and support have been a blessing to me in so many ways. Words cannot explain how honored I am to call you my friend, sister, and mentor may God's blessing rest upon you and your family always.

My personal thanks and gratitude to Kelly Lapp my editor for expressing exercise tact and diplomacy when reviewing the manuscript. Also for helping, me put my voice in print.

Finally, I would like to acknowledge and thank . . . Everyone who has supported me in this project.

Foreword

As a co-laborer in the gospel, I am honored to scribe and submit the foreword for my sister in the Spirit, Pastor Angela Hood She has proven herself an honorable vessel, with a drive and passion to acquire the things of God. I found the information within the pages of *It's Your Life*, to be applicable to daily living for the believer. This book is full not only of information but also instruction that will spark a fire in the reader to check the functionality of their own spiritual artillery. We are reminded through Pastor Angela's straightforward approach to wake up and acknowledge that there is a battle going on. Further, we are challenged to utilize the weaponry we already have in order to win ultimate victory over an enemy that is already defeated.

Written with an urgent tone and subtle sense of humor, you will be ignited and challenged to move defensively toward the onslaught of the enemy rather than running away. Prepare for the spiritual giant in you to be stirred to a position of righteous authority and dominion. In my opinion, It's Your Life is a necessary tool of advancement in the Kingdom. What you now hold in your hands is not just a book, but also an instruction manual that will serve as a reference in your library for years to come.

Joyce Gilmer, DD

Introduction

Then He called His twelve disciples together and gave them power and authority over all demons, and to cure diseases. He sent them to preach the kingdom of God and to heal the sick.

(Luke 9:1-2 NKJV)

"I can still make her my slave, for she does not know how to use her power."

(The Wicked Witch of the West, *The Wonderful Wizard of Oz*)

This book has the ability to change your life. It's not that it is so well-written or so inspiring. No, it is a simple book that expresses a simple truth: you have power. If you are a believer, Jesus has empowered you with spiritual authority. The problem is that most Christians either do not understand the power they have been given, or they do not know how to use the power they have been given. As a result, Christians are still living as slaves to sin and Satan. But it does not have to be that way.

This book will introduce you to the power that you have, and it will instruct you on how to use that power in a Biblical manner. It uses logic and experience – but more than anything, it is full of God's word. As you read, allow God's Spirit to speak to you through His word, for that is the only way that you will discover the life-changing power God wants you to know.

Each chapter spells out everything you need to know about your spiritual authority and then concludes with a section called "Keys to Understanding Your Authority" that summarizes the key points of the chapter and leads you to apply the truths. In addition, each chapter includes "It's Your Turn" questions for you to meditate on and respond to.

You are about to embark on an incredible journey. If you take the truths in this book to heart and apply them to your life, then this could be the beginning of something wonderful that God does in your life.

Section 1

Understanding Your Spiritual Authority

Chapter 1: What is Spiritual Authority?

Authority is defined as the right to control, command, or determine; a commanding influence. It carries with it a right to respect or acceptance of one's word, command, or thoughts.[1] People with authority have both an ability to command and a right to demand respect.

Some people in authority have limited power; they can only command certain people in regards to certain things. Those with limited authority overstep the bounds of their power when they expect obedience from people who are not under their command or when they try to control a situation that is not in their jurisdiction.

Jesus Christ had full authority. He told His disciples, "All authority in heaven and on earth has been given to Me" (Matthew 28:18 NIV). All authority on heaven. All authority on earth. Jesus had the authority to control nature. He had the authority to command demons. He had the authority to teach even the greatest experts. He even had the authority to demand diseases to depart from the people.

The people were amazed by this kind of power.

> "For with authority He commands even the unclean spirits, and they obey Him" (Mark 1:27 NKJV).

> And they feared exceedingly, and said to one another, "Who can this be that even the wind and the sea obey Him" (Mark 4:41 NKJV)?

However, there were some people who demanded an explanation for Jesus' authority.

> Now when He came into the temple, the chief priests and the elders of the people confronted Him as He was teaching, and said, "By what authority are You doing these things? And who gave You this authority" (Matthew 21:23 NKJV)?

Jesus' power was so strong that He could heal people from a long distance away (see Matthew 8:8-13). Power poured from His being to the point that people could simply touch His clothing and be made well from various diseases (see Matthew 14:34-36). The very mention of His name was enough to cause demons to tremble. Jesus had this authority by nature of the fact that He was God. However, He used it for a very specific purpose: to provide salvation for mankind.

> *"No one takes [My life] from Me, but I lay it down of Myself. I have power to lay it down, and I have power to take it again. This command I have received from My Father" (John 10:18 NKJV).*

Unlike Jesus, our spiritual authority is delegated power. We do not have it based on who we are, but based on who He is. Jesus originally gave this authority to His 12 apostles (see Luke 9). In fact, the word APOSTLE[2] means "one sent with authority and a message." He then extended this authority to 70 additional disciples (see Luke 10) and then to all believers (see Mark 16).

Luke 9:1-2 says, "Then He called His twelve disciples together and gave them power and authority over all demons, and to cure diseases. He sent them to preach the kingdom of God and to heal the sick." Let's break these verses apart to understand the authority we have.

First, as already mentioned, Jesus first gave His authority to the 12 apostles, but He later extended the gift to all believers. You have as much right to Jesus' authority as the original 12 apostles had. Let that sink in for a moment. So many Christians sit in weakness and shame because they believe that God does not work today as He did in the Bible. They tell themselves that they are not "special" enough to be used by God – that He only uses preachers and missionaries. If you are one of those believers, check your facts. The men Jesus chose were not special, elite, or unique. They were common: fishermen and tax collectors, brothers and husbands, proud and faithless. Hebrews 13:8 (NKJV) reminds us that "Jesus Christ is the same yesterday, today, and forever." So, the God who chose to work through common people in the past still uses common people today – and He entrusts them with the same power. This authority is yours to claim – no excuses.

The word GAVE[3] in Luke 9 is the Greek word DIDOMI. It means, "to bestow a gift; to give over to one's care, entrust; to give to someone as his own." Understand that the authority you have is a gift. You did nothing to earn it. However, it is more than just a gift: it is also a trust. Jesus entrusted His authority – and with it, His reputation – to your care. He gave you authority to use as your own, but He expects you to use it well. Think of it like a rental house. When you rent from someone else, you claim the house as your own. You live there and use it as you want. However, it is not really your house. It belongs to the landlord or property owner. He expects you to take care of the property – to use it well. He has entrusted it to you, and if something happens, you will have to give account to him. Your spiritual authority is the same way.

So, what exactly did Jesus give us? Power and authority. The Greek word for POWER[4] is DYNAMIS. It means "strength, power, ability, or influence." The word for AUTHORITY[5] is EXOUSIA and it means "power of choice; power of right; the ability one possesses or exercises." Recognize that Jesus gave you power as an ability and authority as a right. You <u>can</u> do what He has said, and you <u>have the right</u> to do what He has said.

And, what exactly did Jesus give you the power and authority to do? We will look at this question in detail later, but to sum it up: You have the power to preach, to heal, and to drive out demons. So many times, we focus on the last two abilities that we lose sight of the first. Yes, you have the power to command demons and diseases – but you also have the ability to preach the gospel. The word PREACH[6] is the Greek word KERYSSO, which means "to herald or proclaim, always with the suggestion of formality, gravity and an authority which must be listened to and obeyed." Jesus gave you authority to proclaim salvation to sinners and liberty to captives. And, He gave you every resource you would need in order to share that good news.

There are some people who will not believe unless they see. There are some people who are so bound by illness or temptation that they cannot believe. There are even Christians who are caught in destructive and controlling strongholds and need to find freedom in a powerful and miraculous way. Jesus gave us the resources we need to reach these people with His love, truth, and liberty. Jesus gave us authority to help these people – to bring healing from physical, emotional, and spiritual diseases and to bring freedom from Satan and his forces. The ability to preach the good news is just as important and exciting as the ability to cast out demons and cure diseases. In fact, it is the reason we have the other powers.

KEYS TO UNDERSTANDING YOUR AUTHORITY

Peter told the blind man in Acts 3:6 (NKJV),

> *"Silver and gold I do not have, but what I do have I give you: In the name of Jesus Christ of Nazareth, rise up and walk."*

But what I do have . . .
We only have as Jesus gives. We do not have unlimited or discretionary authority. We only have the authority and the power to use as He wills and for His purposes.

I give you . . .

However, Jesus gives it so we will use it. Too many of us sit on our authority. We hold it in our pocket like a special treasure. Jesus gave to us so we would give to others: "Freely you have received, freely give" (Matthew 10:8 NKJV). Jesus gave us the authority to do it ourselves, not the command to ask Him to do it. We have to stop thinking that God is going to send down a special miracle here to the earth realm. No! When Jesus said, "It is finished" in John 19:30 that meant everything we would ever need and everything we would ever want have been taken care of for us. Our sicknesses have been taken care of, our struggles have been taken care of and our difficulties have been taken care of. Jesus expects us to use our authority.

In the name of Jesus Christ of Nazareth . . .

Jesus gave us authority as an extension of His reputation and of His ministry. We have the <u>right</u> to exercise authority – but only in His name. As Christians, we have been given the right to use His power, but we must never forget that we also bear His name. What we do reflects back on Him. We must also remember that Jesus expects us to use His authority in order to build His kingdom. Authority over demons and diseases goes hand-in-hand with preaching the gospel.

God is calling you to stand in the power and authority that He has entrusted unto you through the Holy Spirit. Will you?

IT'S YOUR TURN!

1. *How do you feel about the fact that Jesus gave you authority over demons and diseases?*

   _____

   _____

   _____

   _____

2. *What situations or circumstances exist in your life where you could use more of your authority?*

   _____

   _____

   _____

   _____

3. *What situations or circumstances hold you back from using your authority?*

   _____

   _____

   _____

   _____

4. *Are you ready to commit yourself to using the authority God has given you as His child and His kingdom worker? If so, write a prayer of confession and commitment below.*

_____

_____

_____

_____

_____

_____

Chapter 2: Who Has Spiritual Authority?

Right before ascending to heaven, Jesus gathered His disciples and told them.

> *"You shall receive power when the Holy Spirit has come upon you; and you shall be witnesses to Me in Jerusalem, and in all Judea and Samaria, and to the end of the earth" (Acts 1:8 NKJV).*

The power that He originally gave to the 12 apostles and then to the 70 disciples, He then gave to any believer who is filled with the Holy Spirit. What does that mean for you?

First, it means that every Christian has spiritual power and authority. Too long in the body of Christ authority has been a position held only by the pastors, the elders or the leaders. That misunderstanding has created a spiritual handicap within the body of Christ. We have spiritual leeches in the church - people who have not learned to stand on their own. They depend on others in order to overcome situations they face in life. They will suck the life and strength out of you if you allow them to simply because they have not been taught that they have authority over demonic influence, over situations, and over choices. Therefore, we find believers who are not able to stand on their own because they do not come to the truth of who they are in God. We must have a clear understanding of what authority means and to whom authority has been given.

The word of God says He has given us power over the enemy, not just the pastor or the leader.

That means that your pastor has authority, and your church leaders have authority, but it also means that you have authority. When you accepted Jesus as your Savior, He filled you with His Holy Spirit and His power.

God has given you spiritual authority. Yes, you with all your issues. You with all the troubles in your marriage. You with all the struggles with your children. You with all the confusion on your job. You with all your doubts and fears. God has given you power, authority and strength over the enemy. Jesus authorized you to act in His stead. The Holy Spirit has been poured into your life. I know this is a hard concept for many of us to grasp. It seems so outlandish that God would allow ordinary people to command demons and cure diseases, but He does.

Several years ago a woman I know named JoAnn was on a mission trip to Brazil, a country known for its dark magic. One night during a church service, a demon-possessed man entered the sanctuary. JoAnn was preaching that night because the pastor was away at an appointment. When she realized what was wrong, JoAnn looked at her interpreter and asked who was in charge to take care of the situation. "You are," the interpreter replied. So, JoAnn looked at that man and tried to figure out what to do. As she was standing there, the man lunged at her and tried to grab her around the throat – but she spoke first. This woman – a 5'3" housewife from a small town in Florida – demanded that the demon depart in the name of Jesus Christ and in the power of His blood. He did. JoAnn would be the first to admit that there is nothing special about her. She is just an ordinary woman, an ordinary Christian. The only thing that makes her different than other Christians is that she chose to be obedient and to trust that God can do what He said He can do. If she had chosen to doubt – or if God had not been true to His word – then she might not be alive today.

Second, the Acts 1:8 promises means every Christian <u>has</u> spiritual power and authority. The power is there. Jesus said, "You <u>shall</u> have power. . ." He did not say, "You might have power." He did not say, "You could have power." He did not say, "You may be capable of possibly having power." Jesus said you have it. The only question is whether or not you will use it.

There are two basic attitudes that come out when someone is placed in a position of authority: humility or pride. We normally think of humility as a good quality, but in this sense, it is more like "humiliation." Humility says, "I don't deserve this" or "I can't do this" or "Maybe God should pick someone else." At best, humility waits until you are enough to use your authority: smart enough, strong enough, faithful enough. At worst, humility forfeits all rights of authority to someone who "deserves" it more.

Pride, on the other hand, says, "Sure, I can do this. I can conquer anything. I'm strong enough. Bring on the big battles." On some level this sounds like the better attitude, but be careful. The proud attitude waits for a big enough battle. The proud figure doesn't worry about little temptations or issues – he saves up his authority for a worthwhile fight.

This attitude pendulum is not only true in spiritual life, but in other areas of life, too. My friend, Kelly, explains authority this way:

> *I taught high school English for five years. When I first stepped into a classroom, I was a 22-year-old intern in a room full of 18-year-old seniors. Talk about intimidating. To make matters worse, I had never been in a high school before – not even as*

a student – since I was homeschooled. I was terrified that my students would not listen to me and would not respect me. I was confident that they would laugh in my face, mock me behind my back, and make life miserable. At that moment, I had several choices:

1. I could back down in humiliation and let them control everything from day one.
2. I could proudly overlook a few "small issues" and wait until a big issue came up.
3. I could establish my authority as the teacher and demand their respect no matter how big or how small the issue was.

On that first day, I somehow sensed that options one and two would not work. Obviously, letting them control the room is not safe or smart. Even if I decided to let some little things slide, they would not take me seriously on the bigger issues because I had never stood in my authority before. Try putting your foot down when you never have before and see how people laugh at you. The only option you have when facing 30 teenagers is to stand firm from the first moment – that is how you gain their respect enough to build a relationship with them.

Anyone who has ever worked with teenagers knows that the first two choices are really not plausible options. Anyone who has ever tried to stand against Satan knows the same thing. You must stand your ground when situations come your way that will try to undermine your authority. Your life will always be filled with challenges and obstacles, but how you choose to overcome them is totally up to you.

To the humble among us: You will never be "enough" to deserve God's power and love in your life. This is not a self-esteem booster, but the truth of the matter is that you will never deserve the goodness of God in your life. Your pastor does not deserve God's authority. Your church leaders and spiritual mentors do not deserve God's authority. You do not deserve God's authority. No one deserves to have His power poured into his life, but He freely gives it as a gift to all of His children. You do not need a special title before you walk in power. You do not need a certain level of spiritual maturity or knowledge before you walk in power. If you wait until you feel like you're "enough", then you will never realize the full extent of who God made you to be.

To the proud among us: The danger with this attitude is that you are setting yourself up for failure. The enemy is a lot stronger than we give him credit for – not impossible to defeat, but stronger than we like to admit. If you can't beat him at a little temptation battle, what makes you think you can face him in a much bigger battle? The Bible warns: "Therefore let him who thinks he stands take heed lest he fall" (1 Corinthians 10:12 NKJV). The reality is if you think you are strong enough, you probably aren't. If you wait for a big enough battle to warrant using your authority, then you will fail miserably.

Let's look at an example from the Bible: The book of 1 Samuel records a battle between the Israelites and the Philistines. These two nations had been in combat for some time, but this chapter records a temporary standstill in the war. The Philistines had a fighter named Goliath, a giant man and a skilled warrior. Goliath made a deal with Israel that he would go hand-to-hand with any warrior they sent to fight him; whatever side won the competition would win the entire war. The stakes were high, and so was the fear. In fact, 1 Samuel 17:11(NKJV) says, "When Saul and all Israel heard these words of the Philistine, they were dismayed and greatly afraid." Grown men trained for war were shaking in their boots. Though they were encamped together in full battle array, the army of Israel eventually fled from the presence of the giant rather than face him.

Enter a young man named David. David was the youngest of eight brothers. At this point in his story, he was most likely around 13-years-old. His background and experience was as a shepherd. He was not old enough or strong enough to be a member of the Israelite army; the only reason he was at the battle that day was because his father sent him on an errand. No one looked at David and saw a skilled warrior – no one, that is, except God.

Take a look at 1 Samuel 17:33-37 (NKJV) –

> *And Saul said to David, "You are not able to go against this Philistine to fight with him; for you are a youth, and he a man of war from his youth."*
>
> *But David said to Saul, "Your servant used to keep his father's sheep, and when a lion or a bear came and took a lamb out of the flock, I went out after it and struck it, and delivered the lamb from its mouth; and when it arose against me, I caught it by its beard, and struck and killed it. Your servant has killed both lion and bear; and this uncircumcised Philistine will be like one of them, seeing he has defied the armies of the living God."*
>
> *Moreover David said, "The LORD, who delivered me from the paw of the lion and from the paw of the bear, He will deliver me from the hand of this Philistine."*
>
> *And Saul said to David, "Go, and the LORD be with you!"*

If David had been a "humble" Christian, he would have stopped at Saul's first comment – if he had offered to fight Goliath at all. David would have believed that he was not enough to go up against the giant. He was too young. He was too small. He was too weak. Instead, look at David's response: "The Lord who delivered me . . . will deliver me." David knew he was not enough, but he did not let that fact keep him from fighting because he knew that God was bigger than the biggest giant. David did not allow his limitations keep him from completing his assignment that was before him. We all have limitations.

If David had been a "proud" believer, he would have rushed into the fight. What bigger battle is there than a fight with a giant where the fate of the entire nation is at stake? But notice something important: God had actually been preparing David for this moment for a long time. This was not David's first fight. David learned how to deal with attacks and opposition while tending to the sheep. Long before David stood face-to-face with a giant, he learned to fight against lions and bears. He knew that God had gifted him with power and strength, and he chose to use it where he was instead of waiting for a big battle.

David was neither too humble nor too proud. As a result, David had the faith he needed when the giant challenged him. He knew that the same God who had delivered him from the wild animals could easily deliver him from Goliath. Though he was young in both age and experience, David relied on the power God had given him. Though he was still unknown, David fought in the power and the name of the Almighty God. The result? The giant fell.

KEYS TO UNDERSTANDING YOUR AUTHORITY

According to Mark 16:17, authority is a sign of a believer. It follows them. In other words, you do not have a choice about whether or not you <u>have</u> authority. Face it: if you are a believer, it is yours. However, you do have a choice about whether or not you will <u>use</u> authority.

Young David grew up to be one of the most well-known and well-loved characters in the Bible. He was the wise king who worked hard on behalf of his people and enlarged their territory. But, David did not start out that way. He started out as a lowly shepherd boy who simply allowed God to use him where he was.

Oh, that we would learn from David's example! Instead, we sit and wait. We wait for the power to pour in. We wait for our faith to grow. We wait for a battle worth fighting. And in doing so, we set ourselves up for failure. Is your church that way? Are you?

Consider which side of this fence you find yourself on. Are you waiting for God to change you into someone worthy enough for such power or strong enough to use the power? Or are you confident that you can face even the biggest battles – and that is why you are waiting for one?

Either way, the problem is the fact that you are waiting instead of trusting God and standing in His authority. You have to <u>act</u> as one in authority even when you do not <u>feel</u> you are one in authority. Then, and only then, will you actually <u>be</u> one in authority.

IT'S YOUR TURN!

1. *Matthew 25:21 (NKJV) says, "Well done, good and faithful servant; you were faithful over a few things, I will make you ruler over many things." What does this verse imply for a "humble" Christian? For a "proud" Christian?*

   _____

   _____

   _____

   _____

2. *Would you consider yourself more "humble" or more "proud"? Why?*

   _____

   _____

   _____

   _____

3. *Do you consider it a sin NOT to use your authority? Why or why not?*

   _____

   _____

   _____

   _____

4. *Would God consider it a sin? If so, confess your sin of waiting and ask God for the attitude you need to stand in His authority.*

   _____

   _____

   _____

   _____

Chapter 3: What Does Spiritual Authority Do?

To truly understand any concept, you need to be able to know both what it is and what it is not. So, in order to best grasp our spiritual authority, let us look at what it does as well as what it does not do.

What does spiritual authority do?

In Luke 9, Jesus gave His apostles the power to drive out demons, to cure diseases, and to preach the kingdom. As previously mentioned, we tend to focus on diseases and demons, but Jesus' priority was preaching. The ability to drive out demons and cure diseases went hand-in-hand with preaching the gospel. He gave us the ability to do one so that we could do the other.

It is vitally important for us to understand Jesus' intention here. We do not just get to cure diseases and cast out demons for the sake of showing off. Remember the reason for our authority is to bring others to salvation – to preach the kingdom. The word PREACH[7] (KERYSSO) is "to herald or proclaim, always with the suggestion of formality, gravity and an authority which must be listened to and obeyed." Jesus' authority means that we can command Satan's forces, but it also means that we can share His love in a mighty and powerful way.

Jesus told His disciples:

> "I saw Satan fall like lightning from heaven. Behold, I give you
> the authority to trample on serpents and scorpions, and over
> all the power of the enemy, and nothing shall by any means
> hurt you. Nevertheless, do not rejoice in this, that the spirits
> are subject to you, but rather rejoice because your names are
> written in heaven" (Luke 10:18-20 NKJV).

Salvation is Jesus' most amazing miracle. It is so easy for us to forget that sometimes, but His first priority is the state of someone's eternal soul. He gave us the gift of healing and the ability to drive out demons, but only so we could find wholeness in Him.

In Mark 2, Jesus was teaching a large crowd when four men brought their paralyzed friend to Jesus. The Bible says that when Jesus saw their faith, He forgave the man of his sins. The religious leaders immediately questioned Jesus about His statement. Jesus responded, "Which is easier, to say to the paralytic, 'Your sins are forgiven you,' or to say, 'Arise, take up your bed and walk'?" Jesus did heal the paralytic man that day, but only "so that you may know that the Son of Man has power on earth to forgive sins" (Mark 2:10 NKJV). The man's soul was more important to Jesus than his legs wcrc.

This is the real gift of spiritual authority. God can show Himself to the world anyway He wants, but He chooses to reveal Himself through us. It is exciting when a housewife casts a demon out of a man. But it is equally exciting – if not more exciting – when God uses my simple story to change someone's life. I am always amazed when I share my salvation testimony and people not only listen to it, but come to Christ as a result of it. So is a young woman I work with. Here is her story:

> *A few years ago during a mission trip to Venezuela, God gave me the opportunity to share some of my life story with a congregation there. As I shared my struggles and issues and how God had brought me through them, God started moving in the hearts of the people. By the time I was done talking, I could feel His healing power fall on that place. I watched as people cried and prayed and reconciled. It was an awesome sight to see under any circumstances, but it was especially incredible to know that God had used my story to bring about that healing. Maybe this is the kind of thing that only amazes people like me – people who know they really have nothing to offer the world. I have wrestled my entire life with feelings of inferiority and insecurity. So, it boggles my mind that God would use me to do anything – but especially that He would use me to advance His kingdom. I am awed when I think of the people God has put me in contact with, when I think of how He never fails to give me just the right words to say, and when I think of the boldness He has filled me with when I needed it the most.*

Jesus is in the business of transforming lives. That is His specialty. He does it first by saving our souls from sin and death. But He does not stop there. Jesus also transforms fishermen into preachers and housewives into missionaries. He takes the shyest kid and gives her a story to tell and the boldncss to tell it. He told His disciples, "Rejoice that your name is written in heaven – now focus on helping others find the way there, too."

Our primary task is to preach the kingdom – to introduce people to the transforming power of Jesus' love. But to assist with that task, we also have the authority to cure diseases and cast out demons.

Interestingly, Jesus tells His apostles to cure diseases and to heal the sick. He is not being repetitive here. The word CURE[8] in Luke 9:1 is THERAPEUO;

it means, "to restore to health." The word HEAL[9] in Luke 9:2 is IAOMAI and it means "to make whole." The word DISEASES[10] translates simply to "an illness or disease", but the word SICK[11] (ASTHENEO) does not refer to a physical ailment but to an emotional or spiritual issue. So, Jesus gave believers the power to bring health to someone who has a disease, as well as the ability to bring wholeness to someone who is weak or powerless.

The word DEMON[12] refers to any demonic, satanic, or evil force. So, yes, we have the authority to drive out demons in the name of Jesus – but we also have the right to command any evil influence to depart. We will look at Satan and his schemes in great detail later, but for now remember that he is not the bad equivalent of God. Unlike God, Satan is not omnipresent, omniscient, or omnipotent. He cannot be everywhere at the same time. Instead, he sends his demons – his fellow fallen angels – to do his work for him. In some cases, the job is so important that Satan does it himself. Regardless of which enemy we are fighting, we are stronger when we stand in Jesus' name. It is enough to cause Satan himself to tremble.

Here's the point: we have every resource we need in order to help people come to salvation. If you meet someone who is possessed by a demon or otherwise caught up in Satan's influence, you have the authority to cast the demon out and command Satan to leave that person alone. Perhaps you will be in a conversation with someone who just can't find Christ because of a physical ailment. Maybe it is a source of anger and bitterness for the person – or maybe it is so debilitating that he truly cannot understand what you are sharing. In that case, you have the ability to cure that disease in the name of Jesus.

Here's an example: Several years ago my friend, a woman I know named Misty was sharing the salvation message with a man who suffered from Parkinson's disease. As she shared the story of Jesus, the man became quite agitated. He started to ask questions about diseases and why God would allow someone to have such a debilitating illness. No matter how Misty tried to direct the conversation back to the man's need for forgiveness, he managed to bring it back to his disease. The demonic spirit within this man was trying to hinder or stop him from being set free by the power of God. Nevertheless, the gift of discernment was working which allowed Misty to see past the demonic influence and to see the need. So, Misty prayed over the man and asked that his disease would go away so that his heart could also find forgiveness and healing. When she opened her eyes, the man was no longer shaking as he had been. He was sitting there, completely calm and completely strong. By the time she left his house, he had also entrusted his soul to Jesus. God enabled Misty to remove every obstacle so that man could focus on the most important thing: accepting Christ.

What does spiritual authority not do?

Spiritual authority is not full discretionary authority. We only have the authority to command on earth what has already been ordained in heaven. In Matthew 16:19 (NKJV), Jesus told His disciples, ""And I will give you the keys of the kingdom of heaven, and whatever you bind on earth will be bound in heaven, and whatever you loose on earth will be loosed in heaven."

The word translated BIND[13] means "to put in bonds, forbid; to restrict or render helpless. The word LOOSE[14] means "to break up, dissolve, or put off." Therefore, we have the power to capture Satan and render him helpless <u>and</u> we have the power to put off all of his traps and snares, to dissolve any hold he has on us. But what is really interesting about this verse is the verb tense. Both verbs – BIND and LOOSE – are used in the perfect passive participle. That means that we are continuing a work that was completed in the past. In other words, we are simply doing on earth what He has already done in heaven.

Yes, we have power and authority – but do not forget that it is delegated authority. You do not have free reign to do whatever you want. Trying to use your authority for anything other than God's intended purpose can result in it being found useless. It is not that God takes away that gift, but He will not uphold your request if it does not match His will. However, if we are in line with His perfect plan, then God will allow what we allow and He will stop what we stop. That is the promise He gave along with His authority and power.

Here are a few other things that spiritual authority is not and cannot do:

- Spiritual authority is not an action game.
- Spiritual authority is not a virtual reality scene from a movie.
- Spiritual authority is not a magic wand.
- Spiritual authority is not a fairy-tale, a doper's chemical fantasy or a child's naïve wish.
- Spiritual authority is not a prize you can earn, nor is a force you can call upon; without any preparation or thought about its source.
- You cannot use spiritual authority to make people do what you want.
- You cannot make your girlfriend like you or make your husband buy you a new car.
- You cannot make your boss give you a raise or make your co-worker finish your job.
- You cannot use it to hurry up the line in the restaurant or make the teacher change a failing grade.
- You cannot use spiritual authority to destroy God's house.

In spite of what the devil says, you cannot win if you try to turn it against the will of God. You will only hurt yourself.

KEYS TO UNDERSTANDING YOUR AUTHORITY

Using your spiritual authority starts with understanding, what your authority is able to do. While God promises to bind and loose what we bind and loose, He is not obligated to come through on that promise if we are misusing our power. Never forget that God's greatest priority is to change hearts in order to wipe away sins and restore relationship with mankind. While we can do many things with our spiritual authority, that should also be our greatest priority.

IT'S YOUR TURN!

1. How do you feel when you realize that your name is written in heaven?

   _____

   _____

   _____

   _____

2. Do you consider the ability to preach boldly as amazing as the ability to cast out demons and cure diseases? Why or why not?

   _____

   _____

   _____

   _____

3. Can you think of a situation where someone might need some powerful assistance in order to find salvation?

   _____

   _____

   _____

   _____

4. What needs to be bound (put in bonds and rendered useless) in your life? What needs to be loosed (put off and dissolved) in your life?

   _____

   _____

   _____

   _____

Chapter 4: What Do I Have Spiritual Authority Over?

The question we must ask ourselves is: what do I rightfully have authority over? Remember, Jesus has full authority, but we only have limited, delegated authority. We do not necessarily have the freedom to exert our power in every area of life. So, where can you exert your authority?

There are several types of authority:

1. Natural
2. Civil
3. Spiritual

Natural authority is the ability to control nature: land, plants, and animals. Now, obviously, we do not control nature in that it does our bidding. I cannot command tornadoes or hurricanes. However, we do have dominion over the natural world. God gave us this authority at creation:

> *So God created man in His own image; in the image of God He created them; male and female He created them. Then God blessed them, and God said to them, "Be fruitful and multiply; fill the earth and subdue it; have dominion over the fish of the sea, over the birds of the air, and over every living thing that moves on the earth." And God said, "See, I have given you every herb that yields seed which is on the face of all the earth, and every tree whose fruit yields seed; to you it shall be for food" (Genesis 1:27-29 NKJV).*

Being made in the image of God means having dominion over creation. This same verse in the Bible translation called *The Message* explains that we were created to reflect God's nature. Since He has authority, we also have authority. We are to be earthly representatives of the kingdom of God, with power and authority. We are to rule and dominate the earth. God gave us land, plants, and animals for shelter, food, and companionship. He expects us to use nature in order to provide for and protect ourselves. However, part of having natural authority means using our resources wisely. While the earth is here for our benefit, it will not always be useful if we do not learn how to take care of it.

Civil authority is power over people. Though this authority is God-given, it is not universal. In other words, anyone in a position of civil authority (president, governor, king, prime minister) is placed there only because God allows it. However, we do not all get to be president. Most of us have civil authority over a certain group of people by nature of being in a leadership position: pastors have authority over church members, teachers have authority over students, and managers have authority over employees. That leader has the power to control that group of people – but that leader cannot go to any group of people and demand respect or command actions. There is a limit to our civil authority.

While we might not have authority in every civil situation, we certainly can have influence there. Each area of authority also has systems and structures. So, within the civil realm, you also have the political system, the economic system, the social system, and the cultural system. I might not be able to demand and command these systems, but I can influence them. I can shine the light of Jesus into the darkness that Satan has created. We can bring about change. That is our right.

Mankind has a God-given natural authority that is given to us at birth. Spiritual authority is also God-given, but this authority is given to us at rebirth. Every human being has natural authority, but only that people who have been born again into God's family have spiritual authority.

When we think of spiritual authority, we tend to first think of rebuking the devil – but that is just a small part of it. Spiritual authority is actually power over angels, demons, and flesh.

We have been given a charge over our enemy – both his influence in other people's lives as well as his work in our own lives. True authority is being able to take control over our own lives – over our flesh – through the blood of Jesus. Therefore, we can live victoriously; we do not have to give into the temptations that gratify the flesh.

We will consider this topic more later when we look at understanding God's enemy, but for now let us remember that Satan most often fights against us by tempting us to live carnally instead of spiritually. Very rarely does Satan attack us with "big" issues such as demon-possession or dark influence. He does not even tempt us frequently with "big" sins – ones that are outward and destructive. Instead, Satan works against us in very subtle ways, seeking to take our attention and devotion away from God.

The problem is we are too busy living according to the old man—or that old nature—that we don't have a clue as to who we are in God. We must realize that the life we live as a Christian is no longer our own, but we have been bought with a price. We have received Jesus Christ as our Lord and Savior, and therefore the dominion and authority that we lost has been given back to us. We have been given a better way. We should not act and live as if we are still under the control and dictates of the devil.

Take this example from Scripture:

> *Brothers and sisters, in the past I could not talk to you as I talk to spiritual people. I had to talk to you as I would to people without the Spirit—babies in Christ. The teaching I gave you was like milk, not solid food, because you were not able to take solid food. And even now you are not ready. You are still not spiritual, because there is jealousy and quarreling among you, and this shows that you are not spiritual. You are acting like people of the world (1 Corinthians 3:1-3 NCV).*

Paul wrote to the Corinthian church that they were still babies in Christ – they had not grown at all in their faith. They were living according to the flesh, not according to the Spirit. But notice what their issues were: jealousy and quarreling. These people were not being brought down by pornography or stealing. No, they were just bickering. But, Paul told them that such behavior made them no better than the people in the world. The New King James Version says they were acting like "mere men." Paul knew they were better than their natural instincts, but Satan was using that envy and division to ruin their testimonies.

So, Paul gave them a stern reminder:

> *Do you not know that you are the temple of God and that the Spirit of God dwells in you? If anyone defiles the temple, God will destroy him. For the temple of God is holy, which temple you are (1 Corinthians 3:16-17 NKJV).*

In other words, Paul told the believers, "Stop acting like babies and grow up. God's Spirit lives inside of you, so you have no excuse for giving in to this childish and carnal behavior." We would be wise to remember that same warning. God gets angry when His temple is dirtied – but He also gave us every resource we need to overcome Satan, his demons, and our flesh. We are left without excuse.

But that does not mean that controlling the flesh will be easy. Later in his letter, Paul told the Corinthians, "I discipline my body and bring it into subjection, lest, when I have preached to others, I myself should become disqualified" (1 Corinthians 9:27 NKJV). Paul knew how slippery carnality can be, so he beat his flesh into submission so that Satan could not tarnish his witness in any way. We would be wise to follow his example.

KEYS TO UNDERSTANDING YOUR AUTHORITY

When you were born, you received authority over nature, to use the land to meet your needs. When you were born again, you received authority over the spiritual realm. You may command angels and demons as your needs demand. However, you also have dominion over your flesh. Because of that authority, you have the responsibility to make sure that your flesh does not overpower the working of the Spirit inside you. Your testimony and the witness of the entire church rest on you keeping your flesh under control.

IT'S YOUR TURN!

1. What are some ways that you use your natural authority?

_____

_____

_____

_____

2. If you have been blessed with civil authority, how can you influence that system for Christ?

_____

_____

_____

_____

3. Take an honest look at yourself: How are you doing when it comes to controlling your flesh? Why do you think it is so important that we learn to use our authority over ourselves?

_____

_____

_____

_____

_____

_____

_____

_____

Chapter 5: Why Do I Have Spiritual Authority?

This particular question can be taken two different ways, and we are going to look at each one.

Why do _I_ have spiritual authority?
Why would God choose to share His authority with humans – with the church?

Why do we have spiritual authority? We were created in the beginning to rule and have dominion over everything except God. We enforce God's original plan in the Earth realm. Now, why God chose that system, I will never completely understand – but He did choose it, so He is obligated to work with it. God ordained that mankind would carry His image, and His authority goes with that.

While God's exact reasoning might remain a mystery, I can speculate as to why God would impart His image, His name, and His authority to mankind. First, because there is an unseen world watching what takes place on earth. As Philip Yancey explains in his book _Disappointment with God_,[15] "What seems like an ordinary action in the seen world many have an extraordinary effect on the unseen world. We are God's 'Exhibit A', His demonstration piece to the powers of the unseen world."

Yancey uses the story of Job to point out the effect that one man's life can have on the spiritual realm. Satan accused God of blessing Job in order to earn his love. He insisted that Job would not live in love and obedience to God if God removed some of that blessing. In turn, God staked His entire reputation on the fact that Job would not desert Him even if his life circumstances were awful. While Job was sitting in ashes and dust wondering what he had done wrong to deserve such devastation, God and Satan were in all-out combat. Job questioned God and yelled at God, but Job never stopped believing in God – and that is what made the difference. Job came through for God and put Satan in his place simply by believing.

That same spiritual world is still watching today to see the power of God at work in mankind. Every single act of faith is a battle won in the heavenly realm.

But, there is also a seen world that is watching, and God has given us authority in order to prove His love and power to the physical realm. Throughout the first half of his book, Yancey explains how God worked with various people, desperately trying to form a relationship with mankind. Most of us sit in wonder at the miracles God performed in the Old Testament, and we question why God does not seem to work that way anymore. But, Yancey points out that "no pyrotechnic displays of omnipotence could make [people] trust and follow Him." No matter what amazing acts God performed, the people still did not seek Him and love Him. So, God found a different way.

God now entrusts believers with His name, with His power, and with His love. He changes us and then allows us to take part in changing other people's lives. He uses our pasts and our imperfections to prove to the world that He is powerful and that He is gracious.

> *When they saw the boldness of Peter and John, and perceived*
> *that they were uneducated and untrained men, they marveled.*
> *And they realized that they had been with Jesus (Acts 4:13*
> *NKJV).*

Tommy Tenney says, "A man with an experience is never at the mercy of a man with only an argument."[16] God doesn't just give us theology and doctrine because no one will listen to that – no one will be changed by that. Instead, God gives us a story. He gives us a testimony. And then, like Peter and John, He gives us the power and the boldness to share our story. And when we do – when people realize that we are just normal people changed by an extraordinary God – then people marvel. People pay attention. And people end up changed.

<u>Why</u> do I have spiritual authority?
What does God intend for me to do with it?
The Lord Jesus Christ has delegated His power to us through His blood by the inward working of the Holy Spirit. But, <u>why</u> did Jesus give us authority? What does He intend for us to do with it? Quite simply, He expects us to represent Him and His kingdom. While that sounds like a simple task, it is not. See, God does not just want us to represent Him – He wants us to represent Him <u>well</u>. That is the hard part of having delegated authority.

Remember that authority over demons and diseases goes hand-in-hand with preaching the gospel. The heart of Jesus is for the world to accept His grace and salvation. When we represent Jesus well, when we use our authority correctly, people see a Jesus that they want to know. But when we represent Jesus poorly, when we give in to our flesh and pride, then people see that Jesus. Jesus gave you spiritual authority so that you could help other people find Him. Nothing breaks His heart more than when you get in the way of people who need Him.

Philip Yancey explains: "The watching world judges God by those who carry His name. When God 'makes His appeal through us' He takes an awful risk: the risk that we will badly misrepresent Him." And yet, God still chooses to make His appeal through us, to allow us to represent Him, His kingdom, and His heart.

KEYS TO UNDERSTANDING YOUR AUTHORITY

The right use of spiritual authority will give God glory. It will bring Him pleasure and joy. The right use of spiritual authority will change the focus to Jesus, not to you and not to the enemy. The right use of spiritual authority will bring joy to the people. Proverbs 29:2 says that when the righteous are in authority the people rejoice. Did you hear that? When you and I take our place in God and do not give place to the devil and his demonic influence, the people rejoice.

But what happens when we misuse our authority, when we represent God badly? Obviously, God does not receive the glory and Jesus is no longer in focus. And the people? Instead of feeling joy, they will feel despair and hopelessness. After all, we are God's hands and feet on this planet. When we fail to live up to His name, what does that tell people about God?

IT'S YOUR TURN!

1. What does your life tell the unseen (spiritual) world about your God?

_____

_____

_____

_____

2. What does your life tell the seen (physical) world about your God?

_____

_____

_____

_____

3. Are you guilty of badly representing God and His kingdom? If so, write a prayer of confession seeking God's forgiveness for damaging His reputation. Think of specific changes that need to take place for you to carry His name well, and commit yourself them.

_____

_____

_____

_____

Chapter 6: Why is My Authority Not Working?

God works in the spiritual realm. Whether or not we see it in the physical realm is dependent on us, not Him. Typically, if you are not experiencing spiritual power in your life it is either because you are not using your spiritual authority at all or you are using your spiritual authority incorrectly.

Lack of Knowledge

Some people are not living in the power and authority of the Spirit simply because they do not know they have it. So, in case you have made it this far still wondering, let's clear things up: If you are a Christian, you already have authority. It is in you. You just need to use it.

Some people might be aware that they have authority, but they are not exactly sure what it is or how to use it. That is the purpose of this book, but the reality is that God gave you instructions for His authority in His word. We keep asking God for guidance when He has already given it. He had already explained what authority you have and how He wants you to use it. You do not need to ask God if He wants you to tell people about Him. You do not need to ask God if He wants you to cast out demons. You do not need to ask God if He wants you to take a stand against the devil. He has already answered those questions.

Many times we ask God to do something that He has already done. I hear people say all the time, "I wish the Lord would save my husband." What some people do not understand is that they are asking God to do something He has already done. The Bible teaches us that salvation is available to everyone; however, not everyone will receive salvation. Jesus' death on the cross means we <u>do not</u> have to ask God to save anyone; all we have to do is <u>thank God</u> that they are saved and pray that they receive the free gift of salvation and <u>stand</u> on that until it comes to pass!

Remember, we have the keys to the kingdom – to bind and loose on earth what has already been bound and loosed in heaven. It has already been done; we just have to activate it on earth through faith.

Lack of Concern

Sadly, some people know they have authority, but they refuse to use it. After all, while it is awesome to see God work through you, it also typically costs something. It requires you to make a stand in some way – and some people would rather not be bothered by that. Some people are just fine the way they are. There is not a lack of knowledge or a lack of power; it is simply a lack of concern.

This apathetic attitude is so sad, but it is also very common. Many Christians walk through life day after day content just "doing their thing." They are afraid of anything that might rock the boat, anything that might unsettle things – even if it is the opportunity to see God Himself work in an awesome way.

Lack of Belief

Perhaps the biggest stumbling block to spiritual authority is a lack of belief. The Bible says that God cannot and will not work where there is no belief (see Matthew 13:58 and Mark 6:5). Read that again: God <u>cannot</u> and <u>will not</u> work where there is no belief. God demands that we have faith because He needs us to have faith. When God limited Himself to working through mankind, He also set a faith requirement. As a result, He cannot do mighty works where there is no faith. It is not that the all-powerful God can't do something, but He chooses to limit Himself to work within the boundaries of our faith.

When we give in to unbelief, it is either because we do not believe God's power or we do not believe His love. Our minds tell us either "He can't" or "He won't" – or sometimes both. But, how small is your God if He can't protect and defend His people? He created the universe. He parted the Red Sea. He commands the oceans. But, He can't fix a marriage? He can't heal an illness? He can't work through you?

And, how mean is your God if He won't come through on behalf of His children? God delivered His people from bondage in Egypt. God sent His own Son to die in order to conquer sin and death. God wrote your story down before anyone else even thought of you. But you don't think He will defend you against Satan? You don't think He wants to set you free from bitterness, anger, or insecurity? You think He wants to see you fail?

When we really stop and think about it like that, unbelief makes no sense at all. When we really step back and look at it, unbelief turns our God into a weak and mean entity instead of the powerful, loving Father He really is. Why would we serve a God who promises but never delivers? Why would we serve a God who sets us up for failure and shame? In your unbelief, that is exactly what you expect from God. But, why do you think He would do that to you?

God chose to limit Himself so that we could see how much He loves us. He does not need us; He does not need our faith. He could wipe out Satan and his forces with just a thought. But, God wants to use us. He wants to share that experience with us. God is doing something awesome in the world, and He invites us to be a part of it. But that means He will only work if you choose to believe and trust Him.

The good news is that it does not take much faith in order to activate God's power.

> *And when they had come to the multitude, a man came to Him, kneeling down to Him and saying, "Lord, have mercy on my son, for he is an epileptic and suffers severely; for he often falls into the fire and often into the water. So I brought him to Your disciples, but they could not cure him."*
>
> *Then Jesus answered and said, "O faithless and perverse generation, how long shall I be with you? How long shall I bear with you? Bring him here to Me." And Jesus rebuked the demon, and it came out of him; and the child was cured from that very hour.*
>
> *Then the disciples came to Jesus privately and said, "Why could we not cast it out?"*
>
> *So Jesus said to them, "Because of your unbelief; for assuredly, I say to you, if you have faith as a mustard seed, you will say to this mountain, 'Move from here to there,' and it will move; and nothing will be impossible for you (Matthew 17:14-20 NKJV).*

Mustard seeds are actually quite small – so even a little faith is enough to move mountains. What would happen in your life if you just believed God a little bit? What might He be able to do in your job, in your family, or in your heart? What mountains might move? What walls might tumble down? What demons might be cast out?

The other piece of good news is that God can increase your belief.

> *Jesus said to him, "If you can believe, all things are possible to him who believes."*
> *Immediately the father of the child cried out and said with tears, "Lord, I believe; help my unbelief" (Mark 9:230-24 NKJV)!*

Perhaps you struggle with unbelief. Perhaps even faith the size of a mustard seed is hard for you to find. That's okay. Ask God for more. Ask Him to take away your unbelief and fill your heart with belief. He is happy to answer that prayer. As we discussed before, you do not need to wait until you are strong in your faith, you just need to start where you are.

I gave birth to my daughter at the age of 22. She was born 20 weeks into the pregnancy and weighed 15 ounces. The doctor told me I needed to prepare for her funeral because she was not going to make it past 72 hours. I was very young in the Lord at that time. I only knew two scriptures and that was the woman with the issue of blood and blind Bartimaeus. I had no idea or understanding about spiritual authority and the need to take authority over my own situations. However, I did have faith. I had faith in God's word. I believed that the word of God would work for me; therefore, I took action. I went to the hospital day in and day out, praying those two scriptures. I could not hold my daughter because she was on oxygen, and they could not take her out of the incubator. As my faith began to grow, I began to learn more about the word of God. I began to put my trust in God because I was willing to make the transition from fear to faith. My daughter is with me now, she has no complications and she is saved.

See, having spiritual authority requires faith, even if it is just the size of a mustard seed.

Lack of Prayer

After Jesus sent the demon out of the epileptic boy, His disciples asked Him why they could not cast out the demon. Jesus responded that their unbelief hindered their power – but He also made another comment. Jesus told the disciples that this kind of demon only came out through prayer (see Mark 9:28-29). So, then, one reason your spiritual authority is not working might be a lack of a steady prayer life.

Just as God does not need our faith, He does not really need our prayers – but He chose to limit Himself to working through us, so a consistent prayer life makes sense. Prayer is what links our hearts and minds with God's heart and mind. Through prayer we catch a glimpse of who He is and what He wants to do in the world. That is necessary information if we are to carry His name and His authority. Plus, God gets to see our hearts, our thoughts, and our motivations. That is necessary information if He is going to trust us with His kingdom secrets.

Think of it this way: You are the owner of a large business with many employees. Your business has important work to do, and that requires you to delegate tasks and authority to different managers. Each manager, then, carries your vision and intentions to the rest of the employees. In essence, those managers represent you. The employees look at those men, but they see you. Wouldn't you want to make sure those men are going to represent you well? Wouldn't you want to make sure they know and understand your desires for your company? Wouldn't you meet with them on a regular basis so that they can be on the same page as you?

That is exactly what God does with us.

Lack of Confession

The last hindrance to spiritual authority is a lack of confession. Sin separates us from God. It literally makes a barrier where God cannot hear us. So, if you feel like your prayers are hitting a wall, it might be a result of unconfessed sin in your life. If you feel a distance between you and God, there might be a sin issue that is creating that distance. Confess it to God and ask Him to remove the filth and the barrier so that you can once again be a conduit for His Spirit and His power.

KEYS TO UNDERSTANDING YOUR AUTHORITY

Many prophets and kings have desired to see what you see, and have not seen it: How the great men of the Old Testament would have longed to see Jesus' ministry and to minister for Him! How David would have loved to see Jesus do the things He did, and how Isaiah would have longed to hear what Jesus said! We have these privileges, but they did not. Imagine, then, how frustrated those men must be to see us not living in the power and authority we have been given.

Perhaps you are not living in your authority because you are not using it at all – either because of a lack of knowledge, a lack of belief, or a lack of concern. Perhaps you are not living in your authority because you are using it incorrectly – either because of a lack prayer or a lack of confession. Friend, you have authority. It is sitting there, waiting to be used. God is wondering why you are living in defeat instead of standing in the authority He has given you. But, you have to use your authority correctly. God is not going to release His power to someone He cannot trust.

See, whatever your limitation is, here is one important fact: All limits point to a lack of a real relationship – a relationship in right standing – with God. God wants to make sure there is no mistake where the power comes from. He needs to know that He can trust you with His authority. So, He wants you to know His word enough to know that you have authority. He asks you to have faith in His power and His love. He demands that you stay active in a confession and prayer life so that your heart can remain tied closely to His. While God is pleased to share His power with you, what is most important to Him is that you have a right relationship with Him.

IT'S YOUR TURN!

1. What limitation is holding you back from using your spiritual authority?

_____

_____

_____

_____

2. How do you feel about the fact that God chose to limit Himself by working through you?

_____

_____

_____

_____

3. If there is any unconfessed sin in your life creating a barrier for God's presence and power, write a prayer of confession below. You can also write a prayer of commitment to living in belief so that God's work is not hindered in your life.

_____

_____

_____

_____

_____

_____

_____

_____

_____

_____

Section 2

Using Your Spiritual Authority

Chapter 7: Become God's Child

The only way you and I can walk in the power of God is by believing and receiving Jesus Christ as Lord and Savior. This is the one and only condition to having spiritual authority. Every human being has natural authority, but only those who are God's children have spiritual authority.

So, how does someone become a child of God? It basically comes down to three steps: admit, acknowledge, and accept.

Admit you have a problem.
It is a cliché statement, but true nonetheless: The first step in recovery is admitting you have a problem. Our problem is sin. Sin is anything you do that does not please the heart of God. There are obvious sins, such as breaking the Ten Commandments, but those are not the only sins. Sins can be things you do that you shouldn't do, or they can be things you should do that you didn't do. Sins can be both actions and attitudes. So, murder is a sin, but so is hatred. Adultery is a sin, but so is lust.

Most of us do not like hearing about our sins. We like to think that we are pretty good people – or at least better than other people. But, that does not really matter in God's eyes. God measures us by a different standard. He does not compare one dirty man to another dirty man to see which one is cleaner. He compares us to His perfection. By that standard, we all come up stained.

> *There is none righteous, no, not one. There is none who understands. There is none who seeks after God. They have all turned aside. All have sinned and fall short of the glory of God (Romans 3:10-12,23 NKJV).*

The important thing to remember is that sins separate us from God. They are filthy and dirty, and a holy, pure God cannot stand the sight of them. As much as He loves you, He detests your sin.

> *But your iniquities have separated you from your God; and your sins have hidden His face from you, so that He will not hear (Isaiah 59:2 NKJV).*

The other important detail about sin is that sin ends in death.

- *There is a way that seems right to a man, but its end is the way of death (Proverbs 14:12 NKJV).*
- *The wages of sin is death (Romans 6:23 NKJV).*
- *Each one is tempted when he is drawn away by his own desires and enticed. Then, when desire has conceived, it gives birth to sin; and sin, when it is full-grown, brings forth death (James 1:14-15 NKJV).*

So, then, we have this problem called sin that separates us from God and leads us to death. What do we do about it?

Acknowledge that only Jesus can get you out of your problem.

Jesus came, lived, died, and rose again so that we could be cleansed from sins and saved from death. He was the perfect sacrifice: He never sinned, so He could give His life in our place.

When we were unable to help ourselves, at the right time, Christ died for us, although we were living against God. Very few people will die to save the life of someone else. Although perhaps for a good person someone might possibly die. But God shows his great love for us in this way: Christ died for us while we were still sinners.

So through Christ we will surely be saved from God's anger, because we have been made right with God by the blood of Christ's death. While we were God's enemies, he made us his friends through the death of his Son. Surely, now that we are his friends, he will save us through his Son's life. And not only that, but now we are also very happy in God through our Lord Jesus Christ. Through him we are now God's friends again.

Sin came into the world because of what one man did, and with sin came death. This is why everyone must die— because everyone sinned. Sin was in the world before the law of Moses, but sin is not counted against us as breaking a command when there is no law. But from the time of Adam to the time of Moses, everyone had to die, even those who had not sinned by breaking a command, as Adam had.

Adam was like the One who was coming in the future. But God's free gift is not like Adam's sin. Many people died because of the sin of that one man. But the grace from God was much greater; many people received God's gift of life by the grace of the one man, Jesus Christ. After Adam sinned once, he was judged guilty. But the gift of God is different. God's free gift came after many sins, and it makes people right with God. One man sinned, and so death ruled all people because of that one man. But now those people who accept God's full grace and the great gift of being made right with him will surely have true life and rule through the one man, Jesus Christ.

So as one sin of Adam brought the punishment of death to all people, one good act that Christ did makes all people right with God. And that brings true life for all. One man disobeyed God, and many became sinners. In the same way, one man obeyed God, and many will be made right. The law came to make sin worse. But when sin grew worse, God's grace increased. Sin once used death to rule us, but God gave people more of his grace so that grace could rule by making people right with him. And this brings life forever through Jesus Christ our Lord (Romans 5:6-21 NCV).

The hard part with this step is acknowledging that Jesus is the <u>only</u> way to get out of the sin problem. Just as we don't like admitting we have a problem, we also don't like acknowledging that we can't get ourselves out of it. We prefer to do good things or go to the right places (like church) in order to appease God and earn our spot in heaven. But, there is a problem with that: you are stained. No matter what you do or how hard you try, you cannot clean yourself. The Bible says that the best you can offer God – the cleanest thing you can give Him – is still a filthy rag compared to His goodness.

But we are all like an unclean thing, and all our righteousnesses are like filthy rags (Isaiah 64:6 NKJV).

God demands perfection – but He also provided perfection through Jesus. Jesus' death satisfied God's demands. His blood was sufficient and His sacrifice was enough. There is nothing that you can do and nothing more that you need to do. Jesus paid the price. We cannot get authority in any other name; we cannot obtain salvation in any other name. Only in the name of Jesus Christ can any of this be obtained.

Accept His gift.
The only thing that you do to become God's child is accept His gift. He offers you forgiveness, mercy, and love. He invites you to become a member of His family and a citizen of His kingdom. All you have to do is accept that on His terms.

It is not enough to believe in Jesus. The Bible says in James 2:19 (NIV), "You believe that there is one God. Good! Even the demons believe that—and shudder." Many people believe in Jesus. Accepting His gift means receiving Him. It means beginning a relationship with Him. It means turning your life over to the One who died in your place.

> *If you declare with your mouth, "Jesus is Lord," and if you*
> *believe in your heart that God raised Jesus from the dead,*
> *you will be saved. We believe with our hearts, and so we are*
> *made right with God. And we declare with our mouths that we*
> *believe, and so we are saved (Romans 10:9-10 NCV).*

You become God's child through adoption. He has already done all of the work necessary to make you His. The only question that remains is whether or not you will let Him. He did not choose you because of what you can do for Him. He does not ask that you earn your way into His love. He offers Himself freely. He offers salvation freely. Will you say yes to Him?

KEYS TO USING YOUR AUTHORITY

If you are not sure about your relationship with Christ or if you don't know Him, I would like to give you the opportunity to do so. In a moment you will have the opportunity to pray a prayer that admits your problem, acknowledges Jesus' sacrifice and accepts God's gift. But remember that these are not magic words. What matters is your heart. If you say these words without meaning them, then they are just words on a page. But, if you truly mean them – if you are really asking God to save you – then these words will become life to you.

So, if you are ready to accept God's gift of salvation and become His child, then talk to Him. Pray this prayer or one like it in your own words.

> *Father, in the name of Jesus I come before You just as I am.*
> *I ask that You forgive me of all of my sins. I believe in You,*
> *Jesus. I believe that You died for me, and I believe that one*
> *day You will return for me. I ask that You come into my heart*
> *and save me. I receive You as Lord of my life, and I receive*
> *Your forgiveness. Thank You, Jesus, for saving me. AMEN!*

If you prayed that prayer from your heart, you are now saved. You are now a child of God, an heir of His kingdom, and a manager of His authority.

IT'S YOUR TURN!

1. Briefly write your story of when and how you accepted God's gift of salvation.

   _____

   _____

   _____

   _____

2. Whether you became God's child today or a previous day, write a prayer of gratitude to God for saving your soul and making you His child.

_____
_____
_____
_____
_____
_____
_____

Chapter 8: Accept God's Love

Spiritual authority is yours the moment you become God's child, but it doesn't come just because you say you are saved. Even though salvation is a requirement for spiritual authority, demons are not afraid of you just because you are born into God's family. A demon is afraid of the believer who knows who he is in Christ. Demons submit to believers who take their rightful spiritual positions and boldly walk in authority.

So what do you need to do? Claim your identity and position. In her book *God Has a Dream for Your Life*,[17] Sheila Walsh explains it this way: "We have an enemy who wants to crush our God-given dreams. He knows that because of the finished work of Christ on the cross, he is powerless against us. But he has one thing on his side: we don't know who we are." As Christians, we have access to all of the power in the world because the Spirit of God Himself lives inside of us, but we can't use that power if we don't know we have it. At the same time, we won't use that power if we don't truly believe we have it. Satan uses our ignorance and our insecurity against us. But we don't have to let him. We don't have to give up our rights as God's children.

Once you receive God's forgiveness through Jesus and become His child, the next step to using your authority is to accept His love. This sounds like an easy thing to do, but it can be very difficult for some people. We recognize that God loved us enough to send Jesus to die for us, but it can be so hard to live in that love on a regular basis: to truly believe that God loves me. And yet, without that acceptance, you will never be able to stand boldly in the authority that God has given you. You will never truly believe that God will defend you against Satan and come through on your behalf if you never truly believe that He really does love you.

Ephesians 1 paints a wonderful picture of the identity of the believer:

> *How blessed is God! And what a blessing he is! He's the Father of our Master, Jesus Christ, and takes us to the high places of blessing in him. Long before he laid down earth's foundations, he had us in mind, had settled on us as the focus of his love, to be made whole and holy by his love. Long, long ago he decided to adopt us into his family through Jesus Christ.*

(What pleasure he took in planning this!) He wanted us to enter into the celebration of his lavish gift-giving by the hand of his beloved Son.

Because of the sacrifice of the Messiah, his blood poured out on the altar of the Cross, we're a free people—free of penalties and punishments chalked up by all our misdeeds. And not just barely free, either. Abundantly free! He thought of everything, provided for everything we could possibly need, letting us in on the plans he took such delight in making. He set it all out before us in Christ, a long-range plan in which everything would be brought together and summed up in him, everything in deepest heaven, everything on planet earth.

It's in Christ that we find out who we are and what we are living for. Long before we first heard of Christ and got our hopes up, he had his eye on us, had designs on us for glorious living, part of the overall purpose he is working out in everything and everyone.

It's in Christ that you, once you heard the truth and believed it (this Message of your salvation), found yourselves home free—signed, sealed, and delivered by the Holy Spirit. This signet from God is the first installment on what's coming, a reminder that we'll get everything God has planned for us, a praising and glorious life.

(The Message)

There are many different blessings that come from being a child of the King, but let's consider three identity markers found in Ephesians 1: you are adopted, you are accepted, and you are adored.

You are Adopted

The beautiful thing about adoption is that is involves a choice. Adoptive parents choose to receive their child and choose to love their child. It's not just a matter of "You are here, so I love you." Adoptive parents basically say "I choose to take you into my home so that I can love you." They choose to both initiate and complete the relationship. God is the same. He is an adoptive Father – and He chose you.

This is a slippery slope, so stick with me closely. Before God ever laid the foundations of the world, you were chosen and your life in Christ was determined. That does not mean that God chose you for heaven and sent someone else to hell. If He had, then He would not be love. Love, by nature, must involve choice. God freely allows everyone the opportunity to know Him and to receive eternal life. Consider these verses:

> *That faith and that knowledge come from the hope for life forever, which God promised to us before time began. (Titus 1:2 NCV)*
>
> *The Lord is not slow in doing what he promised—the way some people understand slowness. But God is being patient with you. He does not want anyone to be lost, but he wants all people to change their hearts and lives. (2 Peter 3:9 NCV)*

God created the possibility for eternal life for mankind before He created mankind. The word TIME[18] in Titus 1:2 is the Greek word AIONIOS. It means "that which has always been and always will be." As the Thayer Lexicon explains, we have "a gospel whose subject matter is eternal – the saving purpose of God adopted from eternity." God knew from the very beginning that mankind would choose to reject Him – and He gave us that choice – but He also created a way for us to rejoin Him in eternity. He offers that way back home to every single person born on this planet, and His heart breaks every time someone dies without accepting that way. God offers salvation and eternal life to anyone who will accept it – but in His all-knowing wisdom, God knows who will receive Him and who will not.

Now look at that second thought: Your life in Christ was determined. God has already decided who you will be in Christ.

> *For whom He foreknew, He also predestined to be conformed to the image of His Son, that He might be the firstborn among many brethren. Moreover whom He predestined, these He also called; whom He called, these He also justified; and whom He justified, these He also glorified (Romans 8:29-30 NKJV).*

The word translated FOREKNEW[19] means simply "to know beforehand." Again, God knew before He created you whether or not you would choose Him. The word translated PREDESTINED[20] means "to limit in advance." Once you chose to follow God, He limited you to a certain path, a certain focus for your life.

What is the determined path? Look again at Romans 8:29-30. The word CONFORMED[21] means "to be jointly formed." God has determined that you will grow closer and closer to Jesus until you are connected to Him. The word CALLED[22] means "to call by name." God has chosen each of us for a unique calling and purpose. While His path is for everyone to be connected to Jesus, we will all go about that in a different way, through a different calling. The word JUSTIFIED[23] means "to render innocent." Part of God's determined will for your life is that you be found blameless, above reproach, innocent of any wrongdoing. The word GLORIFIED[24] means "to render honorable." God has a place of honor reserved in His heart and His kingdom for those who choose to follow Him and the path He has set out for them.

Again, God chose this path for His children before time began, before the conception of the world. He determined that you would become like Jesus, but that you would do it in a way that is unique to you. He wrote your entire story down before He created light (see Psalm 139). Nothing is accidental. Nothing is surprising to Him.

There are probably multiple reasons why God would choose you and determine a path for you to follow. One reason is simply because He loves you. God chose you to be His holy person in Christ. He chose you to be His child through adoption. That word translated CHOSE[25] in Ephesians 1 means "to pick out or choose for oneself." It carries the idea of choosing one out of many: "I want this one." God said that about you.

God did not choose us because of anything we did. You did not earn your way into His love, and you cannot earn your way out. He chose you because of His purpose and grace.

> *God . . . saved us and made us his holy people. That was not because of anything we did ourselves but because of God's purpose and grace. That grace was given to us through Christ Jesus before time began, but it is now shown to us by the coming of our Savior Christ Jesus. He destroyed death, and through the Good News he showed us the way to have life that cannot be destroyed. (2 Timothy 1:8b-10 NCV)*

The word PURPOSE[26] here means "intention, setting in view." It was the picture God saw in His mind, and He made it a reality. He wanted you, and He wanted you to walk the path He chose. It is that simple. The word translated GRACE[27] here means "that which affords joy, pleasure, delight." God chose your path because it brought Him pleasure – but also because He knew it would bring you joy and delight (see Jeremiah 29:11).

You are Accepted

One of the hardest things for many Christians to realize is that they truly are forgiven and accepted. For some reason, we think that God can completely wash away everyone else's sins but not our own. We continue to give in to feelings of guilt and shame, when God has indeed assured us that we are clean.

Make no mistake: you are a sinner and that sin is filthy in the eyes of God. He knows your sin, your wrongdoing, and your rebellion. He is well aware of every time you have fallen short or come up lacking. He acknowledges your flaws and weaknesses. But that is not the whole story. You are also a dearly loved child of God. He has washed you clean, given you new garments to wear, and has accepted you into His home. Believe that and live that.

One of the most interesting Bible stories to me is Jesus' encounter with the Samaritan woman at the well in John 4. Early in His ministry, Jesus was traveling from Judea to Galilee, and He went through Samaria to get there. One day He decided to rest in the shade of a well while His disciples went into town to get some food. As Jesus was resting, a woman came from the village to draw water from the well. Jesus struck up a conversation with her. During Bible times, Jews and Samaritans were enemies, and men rarely spoke to women in public – so this meeting was odd from the very beginning. As the conversation continued, though, Jesus opened up this woman's life for scrutiny. He told her that she had been married five times and was currently living with a man who was not her husband – a very bad act in those days. But here's what is fascinating about this story: the woman actually appreciated Jesus' honesty. She did not get angry and run away. She did not tell Jesus off. No. He knew her past. He knew her mistakes. But He loved her. He accepted her. And that acceptance and forgiveness changed her life. She immediately ran back to her town and told everyone, "Come and meet a man who told me everything I have ever done."

Now, isn't that interesting? The woman was thrilled that Jesus knew her past. She was so excited by that fact that she brought everyone she knew to meet Him, too. Why? Author Jo Kadlecek[28] explains the Samaritan woman this way: "Her passion for life was suddenly transformed. She became instantly earnest to introduce others – who also knew her past – to this Man. She did not want to show them the error of their ways or some nifty set of values that could magically make their lives better. No, she became focused entirely on bringing the people in her life to see the Man who – of all things – showed her her sin."

What made the difference for this woman? It was knowing that Jesus knew her sin, but loved her anyway. She knew she had done wrong, but she also knew that Jesus had forgiven her. Kadlecek goes on to say, "Of course, not many of us like to be reminded that we are sinful, but when we hear the words from the Person we know is infinite Love, absolute Justice, and unending Grace, the words become for us a soothing balm." There is no shame when Jesus shows you your sin because His love overpowers your guilt. And since there is no shame, there should also be no fear.

So, hear the words of your Father: You are forgiven.

- *Happy is the person whose sins are forgiven, whose wrongs are pardoned. Happy is the person whom the Lord does not consider guilty and in whom there is nothing false. (Psalm 32:1-2 NCV)*

- *As high as the sky is above the earth, so great is his love for those who respect him. He has taken our sins away from us as far as the east is from west (Psalm 103:11-12 NCV).*
- *If we say we have no sin, we are fooling ourselves, and the truth is not in us. But if we confess our sins, he will forgive our sins, because we can trust God to do what is right. He will cleanse us from all the wrongs we have done (1 John 1:8-9 NCV).*

No matter what you have done, you have never been unloved by Him. You have never done something so awful that He can't or won't forgive you for it. And, when God forgives you, it is complete. He takes away the sin, the guilt, and the shame, and He throws it as far as the east is from the west – never to be brought up again. If God is willing to forget it, shouldn't you forget it, too?

To add to the good news: Not only are you forgiven, you are brand new. "If anyone belongs to Christ, there is a new creation. The old things have gone; everything is made new!" (2 Corinthians 5:17 NCV). Your entire life changes the moment you receive God's gift of salvation. You are not the person you once were. Remind yourself of that fact often, and remind Satan every time he comes against you. Whatever you once did is gone. Whoever you were before is changed. You are forgiven. You are new. You are accepted.

You are Adored

It is a lot easier to believe you are adopted (chosen) and accepted (forgiven) when you also know you are adored. So, this is really the key to understanding your identity in Christ. God chose you because He loves you. God forgave you and continues to forgive you because He loves you. Yes, He loves the whole world – but never lose sight of the fact that He dearly and deeply loves <u>you</u>. He created you and chose you for His pleasure. He accepts you as you are: good, bad, and ugly. Face it: you are adored.

God adores you as His creation.
> *You made my whole being; you formed me in my mother's body. I praise you because you made me in an amazing and wonderful way. What you have done is wonderful. I know this very well. You saw my bones being formed as I took shape in my mother's body. When I was put together there, you saw my body as it was formed. All the days planned for me were written in your book before I was one day old (Psalm 139:13-16 NCV).*

If you have ever created something, then you know the pride and love that object brings. Even if you know it is not the best in the world, you would defend it and protect it. Why? Because it is yours. It bears your mark. It reflects your heart. It is part of you. God feels that way about you. You are

His. He formed you just the way He wants you. He placed His image on you. As a Christian, He is recreating you into a reflection of His Son. He thinks you are amazing.

God adores you as His child.

> *Behold what manner of love the Father has bestowed on us,*
> *that we should be called children of God (1 John 3:1 NCV)!*

We talked about becoming God's child in the previous chapter, but remember that you become a member of God's family the moment you accept His gift of salvation through Jesus. The God of the universe had adopted you as His kid. He has obligated Himself to protect you, provide for you, and take care of you. He has promised you good gifts. As His child, you bring joy to the Father's heart. You make Him proud.

God adores you as His friend.

> *No longer do I call you servants, for a servant does not know*
> *what his master is doing; but I have called you friends, for all*
> *things that I heard from My Father I have made known to you*
> *(John 15:15 NCV).*

Those of us who have known God for a while tend to forget how amazing this truth is: You are a friend of God. The Creator of the universe enjoys your company. The Almighty God likes talking to you. In fact, He has promised not only to listen to your concerns, but to share His secrets with you (see Psalm 25:14). That is how special you are to Him.

God adores you as His bride.

- *As a man rejoices over his new wife, so your God will rejoice over you (Isaiah 62:5b NCV).*
- *The Lord your God is with you; the mighty One will save you. He will rejoice over you. You will rest in his love; he will sing and be joyful about you (Zephaniah 3:17 NCV).*

I think this point is slightly more meaningful to women than it is to men, but it is true either way. You are the bride of Christ. You are the object of His affection. You are His completion, His soul mate. Right now, Jesus is preparing a home for you – and someday He is going to come back and take you to that home to live with Him forever. He can't wait to make you His.

I am convinced that life would be different if we could see everyone as God sees them – including ourselves. God is crazy about you. He knows you better than you know yourself, but He still delights in you. That is hard to believe sometimes, but it is the absolute truth. Do you deserve His love? No.

Do you deserve His grace? No. Do you deserve to have His authority? No. But He gives it to you because He wants to.

Perhaps that is the key to accepting God's love: understanding that it is really all about Him. He doesn't adopt you or accept you or adore you because you are worthy of those things. He does it because He is God. He is love. Everything He does is a reflection of His character – His loving character. He does not love you because <u>you</u> are worthy but because <u>He</u> is worthy.

> *But you are a chosen generation, a royal priesthood, a holy nation, His own special people, that you may proclaim the praises of Him who called you out of darkness into His marvelous light (1 Peter 2:9 NKJV).*

Ephesians 1 tells us that the Father chose us to the praise of His glory (vs. 6), the Son redeemed us to the praise of His glory (vs. 12), and the Spirit sealed us to the praise of His glory (vs. 14). See the common thread? Our complete existence is centered around praising His glory.

There are so many times that I know I don't deserve any good thing God gives me. There are so many times that I don't understand why He would do anything for me – let alone why He would do so very much for me. I don't comprehend God's lavish love. But I accept it. If the God of the universe tells me He loves me, then who am I to argue with Him? If He wants to adopt me, accept me, and adore me, who am I to refuse Him?

Who are you to deny Him that privilege?

KEYS TO USING YOUR AUTHORITY

One of my favorite Bible stories is the woman with the issue of blood, which is found in Mark 5:25-34. I love this story because of the unexpectedness of it. Jesus was teaching one day when an important man came and asked Him to come heal his daughter. Jesus immediately agreed and set out for the man's house. But, on the way, Jesus met the woman with the issue of blood. This woman had been bleeding for 12 years. This would have been a huge issue for a woman in that day and in that culture. A flow of blood meant that she could not have children. A flow of blood meant that she would be unclean all the time. Being barren and unclean would have made her a social outcast – an unwanted hindrance.

This woman was obviously desperate. She had been to every doctor around, but no one had been able to help her. As a last resort, she went to Jesus. But, here's how humble this woman was: she did not actually approach Jesus. She simply wanted to touch the hem of his robe because she knew that He was so powerful that even that little touch would be enough to help her. So, as Jesus walked by, the woman dropped to her knees in the dirt and reached out to touch Jesus' garment. Immediately, the flow of blood stopped.

But that is not the end of the story. Jesus, knowing that a miracle had happened, stopped walking and demanded that the person who touched Him come forward. Imagine the shock and embarrassment for that poor woman. Imagine the fear she must have felt when she realized that Jesus knew what she had done.

Jo Kadlecek explains the encounter this way:

> *"Christ did not call her forward to embarrass her, to condemn her, or even to add to the increasing anxiety. He brought her forward because she was* <u>not</u> *insignificant to Him. No one ever is – nor was she bothering Him in the least. Jesus already knew she'd been healed, but He wanted to hold her up as an example of faith, of one who – though she lacked any self-worth – did not allow it to paralyze her belief and acknowledgement of who He was and what He could do. In her, He could show the splendor of His powerful touch, the might of His restoration and healing. And He was in no hurry to do otherwise."*

Just like that woman, you are never a burden to Jesus. He is never sorry to spend time with you or to meet your needs. He loves you and is proud to share His authority with you. Accept that fact. Accept that identity. But remember that He does it for His own glory. He chose you so that He could display His splendor through you. You are the object of His affection, but it is really all about Him.

While that sounds a little depressing, it is actually good news for us. See, your identity is not based on you. It is based on God. So, your identity is as firm as He is. You never have to worry that you will do something to change who you are in God because your identity is about Him. You will be adopted for as long as He exists. You will be accepted for as long as He exists. You will be adored for as long as He exists. Period.

So, when Satan starts attacking your identity, you can remind Him that God adopted you because He wanted you. When Satan makes you question why God would ever use someone with your past, you can remind Him that God accepts you. When Satan makes you feel worthless, you can remind him that God adores you. You can command Satan and his demons to leave you alone – and then you can trust in the authority your Father gave you. He adores you, and He would never let you down.

IT'S YOUR TURN!

1. Why is accepting God's love so important when it comes to using your spiritual authority?

   _____
   _____
   _____
   _____
   _____

2. Which identity do you have the hardest time believing: adopted, accepted, or adored? Why?

   _____
   _____
   _____
   _____

3. How might understanding that it is really all about God help you accept His love?

   _____
   _____
   _____
   _____
   _____

Chapter 9: Understand God's Enemy

You cannot fight an enemy you do not understand. Sure, God has given us authority over Satan and his evil forces, but how do we work against them when we have no clue who they are and what they do? When it comes to Satan, most believers fall into one of two groups: those who over-emphasize him and those you under-emphasize him. Neither group is a good group to be in because neither one is centered on the truth. Our job is to find out the truth about our enemy so that we can best combat him and his schemes.

The History of the Devil

Satan began life as an angel named Lucifer. As with other angels, Lucifer was a created being. That is an important detail because it means that Lucifer <u>was</u> not equal with God, and Satan <u>is</u> not equal with God. As previously stated, there are many people who believe that Satan is the bad equivalent of God - that he has the same power and ability, but uses it for evil instead of good. That is simply not the case. Lucifer was no stronger than any other angel, and he certainly was not as strong as God.

Though Lucifer was not equal with God, he wanted to be - and that desire grew in him until it consumed him.

> *"You were the seal of perfection, full of wisdom and perfect in beauty. You were in Eden, the garden of God; every precious stone was your covering: the sardius, topaz, and diamond, beryl, onyx, and jasper, sapphire, turquoise, and emerald with gold. The workmanship of your timbrels and pipes was prepared for you on the day you were created. You were the anointed cherub who covers; I established you. You were on the holy mountain of God. You walked back and forth in the midst of fiery stones. You were perfect in your ways from the day you were created, till iniquity was found in you."*

> *Ezekiel 28:12-15 (NKJV)*

> *"How you are fallen from heaven, O Lucifer, son of the morning! How you are cut down to the ground, you who weakened the nations! For you have said in your heart: 'I will ascend into heaven, I will exalt my throne above the stars of God; I will also sit on the mount of the congregation on the farthest sides of the*

north; I will ascend above the heights of the clouds. I will be like the Most High.'

Isaiah 14:12-14 (NKJV)

And another sign appeared in heaven: behold, a great, fiery red dragon having seven heads and ten horns, and seven diadems on his heads. His tail drew a third of the stars of heaven and threw them to the earth. And the dragon stood before the woman who was ready to give birth, to devour her Child as soon as it was born.

Revelation 12:3-4 (NKJV)

The name LUCIFER[29] means "Light-bearer" or "Daystar". Lucifer was an absolutely perfect cherub, a guard in the heavenly army. The expression "the anointed cherub who covers" in Ezekiel 28:14 is a reference to his high rank and position. Lucifer was a trusted companion and important officer in the kingdom of God – but that was not enough for him. He wanted to be God. In a heavenly mutiny, Lucifer tried to usurp divine authority, and he convinced one-third of the angel force to fight with him.

Ultimately, Lucifer was expelled from heaven and given the name Satan (which means "adversary"). Satan was cast out of heaven, but he was also cast down to earth. Before time on earth began, God told Satan that there is an eternal pit of fire waiting for him and his minions. Satan has been given a short time of freedom on earth, but he is already completely destroyed – and he knows it. The pit is already prepared for him. Satan cannot beat God, but he can break God's heart by taking God's children down to the pit with him.

Ever since his fall to earth, Satan has had two major objectives: to stop God's redemptive plan and to draw as many people away from God as possible. Since Jesus arrived, died, and rose again, Satan can no longer accomplish his first goal in thwarting God's salvation. So, that means he needs to devote all of his resources to his second goal. Remember that Satan is not as powerful as we think he is, but he has had 6,000 years of focused attention on this one objective. He is bound to be good at it.

The Tactics of the Devil

So, who exactly is this adversary and what is his battle plan? Satan goes by multiple names, all of which give us insight into our enemy:

- Abaddon/Apollyon = Destroyer
- Belial = Worthless one
- Beelzebub/Beelzebul = Prince of devils
- Devil (diabolos) = Slanderer

Satan is also known as a snake (Genesis 3) and a prowling lion (1 Peter 5:8). Jesus called Satan the father of all lies, a thief, and the wicked one. This is definitely an enemy that we need to take seriously.

In addition, we must remember that Satan does not work alone. Ephesians 6:12 tells us that Satan is the prince of the powers of the air, meaning he controls all demons and other evil forces. According to Ephesians 6, Satan and his demons operate in order and rank. You are not fighting Satan if you are a low-level, low-minded believer; you are fighting a demon. If you look in the scripture, Satan never possesses any man. Every person who was delivered by Jesus was demon-possessed not Satan-possessed. There is a difference. Some demonic spirits hold higher rank in Satan's kingdom; therefore, their influence in your life can appear to be a lot stronger depending on where you are in your walk with Christ. The higher you go in Christ, the harder the level of spiritual attack you will come under. Satan himself attacks those who are in high rank and who create a threat to his kingdom.

Let's take a look at some of Satan's tactics:

1. Satan accuses.
   Then I heard a loud voice saying in heaven, "Now salvation, and strength, and the kingdom of our God, and the power of His Christ have come, for the accuser of our brethren, who accused them before our God day and night, has been cast down" (Revelation 12:10 NKJV).

2. Satan afflicts.
   So Satan went out from the presence of the LORD, and struck Job with painful boils from the sole of his foot to the crown of his head (Job 2:7 NKJV).

3. Satan blinds.
   . . . whose minds the god of this age has blinded, who do not believe, lest the light of the gospel of the glory of Christ, who is the image of God, should shine on them (2 Corinthians 4:4 NKJV).

4. Satan buffets.
   And lest I should be exalted above measure by the abundance of the revelations, a thorn in the flesh was given to me, a messenger of Satan to buffet me, lest I be exalted above measure (2 Corinthians 12:7 NKJV).

5. Satan deceives.
   Now when the thousand years have expired, Satan will be released from his prison and will go out to deceive the nations which are in the four corners of the earth, Gog and Magog, to

gather them together to battle, whose number is as the sand of the sea (Revelation 20:7-8 NKJV).

6. Satan ensnares.
   Moreover he must have a good testimony among those who are outside, lest he fall into reproach and the snare of the devil (1 Timothy 3:7 NKJV).

7. Satan opposes.
   Then he showed me Joshua the high priest standing before the Angel of the LORD, and Satan standing at his right hand to oppose him (Zechariah 3:1 NKJV).

8. Satan sifts.
   And the Lord said, "Simon, Simon! Indeed, Satan has asked for you, that he may sift you as wheat (Luke 22:31 NKJV).

9. Satan tempts.
   Then Jesus was led up by the Spirit into the wilderness to be tempted by the devil (Matthew 4:1 NKJV).

Our enemy is serious about attacking us. We should never underestimate the lengths he is willing to go to in order to defeat us. There is absolutely nothing good in him. I sometimes think, "Sure, he's the devil, but he would never go so low as to . . ." In thinking that, I give Satan more credit than he is worth. There is no low too low for him. He has no compassion or sympathy - though he will pretend to if he thinks it will help him deceive me. No matter what he tells you: Satan never has your best interest in mind - he doesn't even have your interest in mind. He is only thinking of himself and his revenge against God.

Remember: Satan does not want to turn you to himself. He does not care if you worship him, care about him, or even acknowledge him. All he really wants is to turn you away from God. Satan will blind you to the truth in order to make it easier to deceive you. He will plant doubt in your mind. He will quietly oppose you or openly beat you. He will do whatever it takes.

We often underestimate Satan because his tactics are sly and understated. Again, he does not want to make Satanists out of all of us - he simply wants to make nonbelievers out of all of us. If you are already a Christian, his best tactic is to ruin your testimony. You might already be sealed for heaven, but he can stop you from helping others find their way. Sometimes Satan attacks our reputations through temptations like alcoholism and pornography – but most of the time he does not need to go that far. More often Satan tears us down with pride, indifference, and distraction.

We also underestimate Satan because we do not often make his job difficult. When Satan first tempted Eve in the Garden of Eden (Genesis 3), it only took one question and one statement to completely turn Eve's heart away from trusting God. He filled her mind with doubt and then denial. That is no different from the way Satan tempts us. Doubt and denial. That is all it takes. Satan's only tool is deception. He has no supernatural power. In fact, the only power he has is what we give him. According to the book of James, Satan uses deception and temptation to entice up away from God and His will for our lives. Most of the time, we do not put up much of a fight.

James also confirms what we already know to be true: Many temptations begin in us. Satan does not use anything new. When he constructs his yokes, there is something already there. The temptation calls to us from within us. We hear that call almost every day, and we've all had the experience of responding to that call. We've all failed to live up to our own standards, to say nothing of God's standards. We must understand that temptations are designed to throw us off course and make us lose our focus. When we lose our God-given focus and get distracted with the world's lust, then we cannot see our enemy coming.

I can remember a time when I was having some issues in my marriage. My husband and I would fight all the time. I got to the point where I would not pray, I did not want to go to church, and all I wanted to do was stay home and cry. During this time, the enemy brought all different types of temptation my way – tempting me to leave my marriage and to give up on everything that the Lord had given me. Satan wanted me to believe that it would be better on the other side; he tried to make his lie a reality by allowing men to come my way who would have sweet words or who would give me a beautiful compliment. The Lord opened my eyes, I began to see the devises of my enemy, and I got to that place like Christ where I began to use the word of God in my marriage and in my own life.

There are three things we must understand about temptation:

1. It is universal – everyone is tempted.
2. It is inevitable – if temptation comes to every person, which it does, then it is inevitable that it will come to us.
3. It is personal – we all have our personal temptations; we are all vulnerable in different ways.

Often, when we are tempted the first thing we want to do is blame God for the temptation. However, James 1:13 says, "When tempted, no one should say, 'God is tempting me' for God cannot be tempted by evil, nor does he tempt anyone." God is not the source of our temptation. To believe that He is the source is a faulty analysis. You see, unless we understand the real source of our temptation, we will respond to it incorrectly. In addition, if we blame God, we certainly will not come to God for help overcoming temptation.

Temptation starts with desire: I look, I see, I want. Moreover, we get in trouble when we allow legitimate desires to dictate illegitimate actions. James tells us that it is our own evil desires that begin this process. Since our desires are very strong and powerful, Satan uses things that we like as bait. While trials are external pressures put upon us, temptations are internal desires. What we fail to realize is that desire leads to sin, and sin leads to physical and spiritual death (separation from God). Satan will make us think his way is best, but only God has the best for us. When God has a blessing for us, Satan will try to offer a cheap substitute.

Remember that Satan tells things that are almost true – things that have some facts or have happened, but he puts a "demonic" spin on them. His lies look good on the outside. They make sense, might work and appear "right", but ultimately they work against the word of God for the devil's purposes. The devil is clever and deceives by something that looks like a good cause on the surface. The devil pretends to give power through hate, anger, frustration, or resentment. Any negative force can be twisted to his benefit. He plants distrust, especially among friends and leaders. If he cannot destroy you, then he will try to make you appear weak and ridiculous.

In addition, the devil rules by fear. He wants to get you angry and then tell you it is hopeless. He wants you to be blind. He wants to cloud the issues and mock the truth and Christ-centered people. He wants to make you feel guilty and think that God will not forgive you, or that God will forgive others but not you. He tells you that you are not worthy and then he tells you that you are so much better and more important than anyone else, even God. He contradicts God, but he also contradicts himself when necessary. He will stop at nothing to confuse you, accuse you, and excuse you. But Satan is a liar!

The Defeat of the Devil

The devil is our adversary, but he is an annihilated adversary. A conquered foe. A defeated enemy. It is vitally important that believers understand, believe, recognize, and know that. Many times Bible teachers say that Jesus defeated Satan through the cross and the empty tomb, but that is not completely accurate. Jesus defeated sin through the cross and death through the tomb, but Satan was defeated before God spoke the world into existence.

> *For you have said in your heart: "I will ascend into heaven,*
> *I will exalt my throne above the stars of God; I will also sit*
> *on the mount of the congregation on the farthest sides of the*

*north; I will ascend above the heights of the clouds. I will be
like the Most High." Yet you shall be brought down to Sheol,
to the lowest depths of the Pit. Those who see you will gaze at
you, and consider you, saying: "Is this the man who made the
earth tremble, who shook kingdoms, who made the world as a
wilderness and destroyed its cities, who did not open the house
of his prisoners?" All the kings of the nations, all of them, sleep
in glory, everyone in his own house; but you are cast out of your
grave like an abominable branch, like the garment of those who
are slain, thrust through with a sword, who go down to the
stones of the pit, like a corpse trodden underfoot.*

Isaiah 14:13-19 (NKJV)

*By the abundance of your trading you became filled with
violence within, and you sinned; therefore I cast you as a
profane thing out of the mountain of God; and I destroyed you,
O covering cherub, from the midst of the fiery stones. Your
heart was lifted up because of your beauty; you corrupted your
wisdom for the sake of your splendor; I cast you to the ground,
I laid you before kings that they might gaze at you. You defiled
your sanctuaries by the multitude of your iniquities, by the
iniquity of your trading; therefore I brought fire from your midst;
it devoured you, and I turned you to ashes upon the earth in the
sight of all who saw you. All who knew you among the peoples
are astonished at you; you have become a horror, and shall be
no more forever.*

Ezekiel 28:16-19 (NKJV)

The minute God cast Satan out of heaven, He had already conquered him and created a plan to redeem His people. God has already defeated Satan, but that is a fact that Satan would like us to forget. He continues to fight against us. But God also gave us the skills and resources we would need in order to gain victory over the devil.

Watch the Enemy

*. . .lest Satan should take advantage of us, for we are not
ignorant of his devices.*

2 Corinthians 2:11 (NKJV)

Satan is prowling around, looking for an opportunity to trip you and trap you. Why not prowl back? He has studied you - so study him. It is Basic War Training 101: Know your enemy. Don't be ignorant of his tricks and schemes. Learn what tactics he uses against you most often, and learn what situations and circumstances make you most open to his lies and temptations. Ephesians 4:27 warns us not to give place to the devil. The word PLACE[30] literally refers to a foothold, a place on a mountain that you grab onto in order to climb. In other words, don't make it easy for Satan to claim victory in your life. He knows your weaknesses and is ready to use them against you. For heaven's sake, figure out what those weaknesses are so that you are not a sitting target. And while you are at it, learn what Satan's weaknesses are, too.

Resist the Enemy

> *Therefore submit to God. Resist the devil and he will flee from you.*
>
> *James 4:7 NKJV*

> *Be sober, be vigilant; because your adversary the devil walks about like a roaring lion, seeking whom he may devour. Resist him, steadfast in the faith, knowing that the same sufferings are experienced by your brotherhood in the world.*
>
> *I Peter 5:8-9 NKJV*

It is possible to resist the devil - and when you start resisting him, you will quickly learn that Satan is a wimp. He really does not like fighting an opponent who fights back. Put your foot down for once and see how Satan runs away. Remember: Satan is not the evil counterpart of God. He cannot be everywhere at once, and he does not know everything. Most of the time, your battles are actually against one of Satan's minions - not against Satan himself. You're not even fighting the master tempter, but a demon that Satan sent in his place. Just resist him. Make the decision not to believe his lies, and you will find that he is powerless against you.

The Bible commands a two-step resistance of the devil: flee immorality and pursue godliness. This is the Biblical strategy for resisting Satan and overcoming temptation. Fleeing immorality means staying out of certain places. The alcoholic must avoid the bar. The drug user must avoid the drug house. The gambler must avoid Las Vegas. But there can be more subtle places to avoid. Someone who struggles with sexual fantasy might need to avoid certain television shows, movies, or books. Someone who struggles with anger needs to avoid situations that rile the temper. Remember that the word is FLEE immorality. <u>Flee</u> temptation. Run as far away as possible. Don't let it come near you. The minute you sense it, turn around and go away.

But, fleeing temptation is only half of the battle. You must also pursue godliness. Fill your life with good, God things. Carefully choose what you watch, who you associate with, and where you go. Fill your mind with God's word so that you know what His will is and so that you can fight Satan when he attacks.

Fight the Enemy

> *Finally, my brethren, be strong in the Lord and in the power of His might. Put on the whole armor of God, that you may be able to stand against the wiles of the devil. For we do not wrestle against flesh and blood, but against principalities, against powers, against the rulers of the darkness of this age, against spiritual hosts of wickedness in the heavenly places. Therefore take up the whole armor of God, that you may be able to withstand in the evil day, and having done all, to stand. Stand therefore, having girded your waist with truth, having put on the breastplate of righteousness, and having shod your feet with the preparation of the gospel of peace; above all, taking the shield of faith with which you will be able to quench all the fiery darts of the wicked one. And take the helmet of salvation, and the sword of the Spirit, which is the word of God; praying always with all prayer and supplication in the Spirit, being watchful to this end with all perseverance and supplication for all the saints.*

> *Ephesians 6:10-18 NKJV*

For the rare occasion when resisting the devil is not sufficient, God has supplied an entire armor for you to use against your enemy. In fact, God promises that you not only can win, but you can come out of the battle standing. So, fight back. Refuse to put yourself in situations where Satan can take control. Pray diligently that the enemy will be bound and unable to work against you. When he comes in armed for a fight, arm yourself with the word of God and blow him away.

Overcome the Enemy

> *Then I heard a loud voice saying in heaven, "Now salvation, and strength, and the kingdom of our God, and the power of His Christ have come, for the accuser of our brethren, who accused them before our God day and night, has been cast down. And they overcame him by the blood of the Lamb and by the word of their testimony, and they did not love their lives to the death.*

> *Revelation 12:10-11*

Finally, don't ever forget that the devil is already defeated. In fact, he is annihilated. The only victory he can have in your life is the victory you give him. He has no right to control your mind or your heart, unless you give him that ability. You can overcome him because God already did.

One vitally important thing to remember about our enemy is that he cannot touch us unless he has permission from God. In Luke 22:31, Satan wanted to sift Simon Peter – to crush him and bring out everything bad in him. But notice that Satan had to ask for the opportunity to sift Peter. He could not do it without checking with God first. And God gave Satan permission. Why? Isn't that a bit cruel? Not at all. See, God knew that Peter could handle the battle - and that he would end up better and stronger as a result. Of course, Peter could not handle the fight on his own, so Jesus added His own power by praying for Peter. Find comfort in knowing that He does the same for you.

KEYS TO USING YOUR AUTHORITY

Satan should not be underestimated, but he should also not be overestimated. He is a cunning enemy, but he is also a conquered enemy. However, that does not mean that we can back off of the battle for a second because our enemy wants to take as many of us out of the war as he can. Instead, we need to watch him, resist him, and fight him so that we can overcome him.

But more than anything else, we need to be in constant awareness that our God is bigger and stronger than any enemy we will ever face. And even better: our God is ultimately more loving than anyone we will ever know. Our Dad in heaven has already beat up the playground bully who likes to torment us. So, when Satan starts to taunt and tease you, tell him to take it up with your Daddy. Then trust your God to come through for you.

IT'S YOUR TURN!

1. What tactic does Satan most often use against you? Do you make his job hard for him or do you give in easily?

_____

_____

_____

_____

_____

_____

2. How does it make you feel to know that your adversary has already been annihilated? How might that knowledge change the way you live?

_____

_____

_____

_____

_____

_____

3. Read Romans 16:20 and write the verse below.

_____
_____
_____
_____
_____
_____
_____
_____

Chapter 10: Know God's Word

In order to walk in authority you must be in obedience to the word of God. You cannot exercise authority if you do not submit to authority; this will only be accomplished when you stand in obedience to the word of God. That is why it is vital for every believer to have a firm foundation in and a clear understanding of the word of God. We can win every battle if we understand the word of God, we can face every giant if we understand the word of God, and we can overcome every trial if we understand the word of God!

Accept its Authority

The term WORD OF GOD refers to both the person of Jesus Christ and the written scriptures (the Bible). Jesus was and is the eternal Word of God, the physical manifestation of God's power and love. The Bible says in Genesis 1 that God created the heavens and the earth by speaking them into existence. But, God did not merely make these things from nothing; He caused them to live. Whatever God releases out of His mouth brings life. When the Lord spoke a word, He spoke it with intent and purpose. In other words, He did not release a word just because He was angry or just because He wanted something to say. God does not work by accident or by chance. He promises that His word will not return to Him void, but it will accomplish what it was sent to do (see Isaiah 55:10-11).

You will never know the power of the Bible until you first accept the authority of the Bible. If the Scriptures are nothing more than historical fables to you, then you will not be able to use them to combat the enemy. The Bible is certainly an important historical book and literary classic. Despite its age, it is consistently at the top of the best-seller lists because it is a book of adventure, romance, history, and poetry. It includes stories about war, passion, and the supernatural. It has endured thousands of years, and has been translated into thousands of languages. But that is not all that the Bible is. Jesus' spoken words have been recorded for us in the Bible – and these recorded words are powerful and purposeful in the life of the believer.

So, just how powerful is the Bible and what can it do for you? Consider these verses:

- *As the rain and the snow come down from heaven, and do not return to it without watering the earth and making it bud and flourish, so that it yields seed for the sower and bread for the eater, so is my word that goes out from my mouth: It will not return to me empty, but will accomplish what I desire and achieve the purpose for which I sent it (Isaiah 55:10-11 NIV).*

The word will accomplish what God sent it to do. When we share God's word, He promises that it will do something. Even if we can't tell right away what that something is, we know that it has a purpose; it will not be empty or pointless.

- *Heaven and earth will pass away, but my words will never pass away (Matthew 24:35 NIV).*
  God's word is eternal; it will never pass away.

- *All Scripture is given by inspiration of God, and is profitable for doctrine, for reproof, for correction, for instruction in righteousness, that the man of God may be complete, thoroughly equipped for every good work (2 Timothy 3:16-17 NKJV).*
  God's word is inspired by God. The word INSPIRATION[31] literally means "God-breathed". Though God used the hands of 40 different writers, every thought and idea came straight from the mind of the all-knowing God. God's word is meant to equip us with everything we need in order to live life God's way.

- *For the word of God is living and powerful, and sharper than any two-edged sword, piercing even to the division of soul and spirit, and of joints and marrow, and is a discerner of the thoughts and intents of the heart (Hebrews 4:12 NKJV).*
  The word is living and active, powerful enough to pierce directly to the heart.

- *Most of all, you must understand this: No prophecy in the Scriptures ever comes from the prophet's own interpretation. No prophecy ever came from what a person wanted to say, but people led by the Holy Spirit spoke words from God (2 Peter 1:20-21 NCV).*
  The Bible is God's word as written down by man, with no human interpretation or mistake. Since it is God's word and not man's, we can rely on it as being without error.

- *I have taken your words to heart so I would not sin against you (Psalm 119:11 NCV).*
  The Bible can keep you from sinning.

- *Your word is a lamp to my feet and a light to my path (Psalm 119:105 NKJV).*
  The Bible can guide you where you should go.

- *So then faith comes by hearing, and hearing by the word of God (Romans 10:17 NKJV).*

  The Bible can lead you to salvation through faith.

- *Finally, be strong in the Lord and in his great power. Put on the full armor of God so that you can fight against the devil's evil tricks. Our fight is not against people on earth but against the rulers and authorities and the powers of this world's darkness, against the spiritual powers of evil in the heavenly world. That is why you need to put on God's full armor. Then on the day of evil you will be able to stand strong. And when you have finished the whole fight, you will still be standing. So stand strong, with the belt of truth tied around your waist and the protection of right living on your chest. On your feet wear the Good News of peace to help you stand strong. And also use the shield of faith with which you can stop all the burning arrows of the Evil One. Accept God's salvation as your helmet, and take the sword of the Spirit, which is the word of God (Ephesians 6:10-17 NCV).*

  The Bible is part of the armor of God that you can defend you against Satan.

- *But if someone obeys God's teaching, then in that person God's love has truly reached its goal. This is how we can be sure we are living in God (1 John 2:5 NCV).*

  The Bible can show you whether or not you belong to God and how He is working in your life.

The Bible is known as the Scriptures or the Word. In the Bible, there are four different words that are translated as WORD: IMRAH (Hebrew), DABAR (Hebrew), REMA (Greek), and LOGOS (Greek). Both Hebrew words and the Greek word REMA refer to a spoken word. The Hebrew words are also translated as *word, speech,* or *commandment.* The Greek REMA[32] can also refer to any utterance of sound, such as a baby crying or an animal noise. The Greek word LOGOS[33], however, is defined as "an expression of intelligence". It refers to a word which embodies an understood idea. Bottom line: the first three words deal with hearing, but LOGOS deals with understanding. In the New Testament, almost every reference to the word of God is a translation of the word LOGOS, which tells us that it is not the words themselves that matter, but the understanding of them.

Is the Bible a life-changing book? It is to those people who take the time and effort to truly understand what it is saying. It is to the people whose eyes have been opened to the truth on its pages. It is to the people whose minds have been changed by the truth on its pages. It is to the people whose hearts have been pierced by the truth on its pages.

> *Since God has so generously let us in on what he is doing, we're not about to throw up our hands and walk off the job just because we run into occasional hard times. We refuse to wear masks and play games. We don't maneuver and manipulate behind the scenes. And we don't twist God's Word to suit ourselves. Rather, we keep everything we do and say out in the open, the whole truth on display, so that those who want to can see and judge for themselves in the presence of God. If our Message is obscure to anyone, it's not because we're holding back in any way. No, it's because these other people are looking or going the wrong way and refuse to give it serious attention. All they have eyes for is the fashionable god of darkness. They think he can give them what they want, and that they won't have to bother believing a Truth they can't see. They're stone-blind to the dayspring brightness of the Message that shines with Christ, who gives us the best picture of God we'll ever get (2 Corinthians 4:1-4 The Message).*

Hide it in Your Heart

Once you are willing to see the Bible as more than just an important historical book, then you are poised for it to transform your life. Now you can begin hiding it in your heart as David did in Psalm 119:11. The word translated HID[34] in that verse is the Hebrew word TSAPHAN. It means to "treasure or store up." Hiding God's word is not just about memorizing it – although that is important. All of Psalm 119 talks about God's laws and commandments being a sweet treasure, a bounty waiting to be discovered. Hiding God's word is about treasuring it, discovering its beauty and richness, and delighting in it.

However, memorizing Scripture is vitally important to fighting Satan's attacks. The word of God is so powerful – even Jesus used it. Right before He began His earthly ministry, Jesus was tempted by Satan after 40 days of fasting. The Bible says in Luke 4:5-13 that when Jesus was tempted by the devil, He answered with the word of God. He stated several times "It is written," "It is written," and again, "It is written." The devil is subject to the word of God!

The one verse in the New Testament that uses the word REMA instead of LOGOS is Ephesians 6:17, which tells us that the word is our sword against Satan's attacks. Isn't it interesting that when fighting Satan we do not need to use an expression of intelligence, but any utterance of sound will do? Is it possible that the word of God is so powerful that all we need to do is speak it and Satan trembles, whether we understand the fullness of what we are speaking or not?

Do What it Says

The Bible is authoritative and powerful. The mere utterance of the word is enough to make Satan flee in terror, and the understanding of the word is enough to change lives for eternity. However, the book of James makes it clear that we are expected to follow the commands of the Bible and not just know them.

> *Do not merely listen to the word, and so deceive yourselves. Do what it says. Anyone who listens to the word but does not do what it says is like a man who looks at his face in a mirror and, after looking at himself, goes away and immediately forgets what he looks like. But the man who looks intently into the perfect law that gives freedom, and continues to do this, not forgetting what he has heard, but doing it—he will be blessed in what he does (James 1:22-25 NIV).*

KEYS TO USING YOUR AUTHORITY

The word of God is power in the life of a believer, but you must learn how to use it but accepting its authority, hiding it in your heart, and doing what it says.

IT'S YOUR TURN!

1. How has the Bible been powerful in your life?

   _____
   _____
   _____
   _____

2. Why is it important to hide the word and do the word?

   _____
   _____
   _____
   _____

3. What does it mean to you that even Jesus used Scripture to fight Satan?

   _____
   _____
   _____
   _____
   _____

Chapter 11: Recognize God's Truth

You desire truth in the inward parts, and in the hidden part You will make me to know wisdom (Psalm 51:6 NKJV).

We live in a world of deception. Society lies to us. Individual people lie to us. We even lie to ourselves. Most of the time these lies are so subtle that we do not even recognize them as lies until we are in too deep. We find ourselves standing at the bottom of a pit wondering, "How did I get here?" Only then can we see the lies that we chose to believe - the lies that Satan threw at us like fiery darts.

The most dangerous lies are the ones we tell ourselves. We tell ourselves lies on a regular basis, but because they come from the heart, we believe them to be true. But, Jeremiah 17:9 (NKJV) tells us, "The heart is deceitful above all things and desperately wicked." If we can't even trust our hearts, then who can we trust?

There is only one person you can trust implicitly: God. And part of standing firm in your authority is learning to recognize His truth through all of the lies. You need to constantly ask Him to tear down lies so that you can see the truth of life. You need to ask God to open your eyes to the big picture so you can see what is truly happening in both the seen and the unseen world. You need to ask Him for boldness to speak His truth. Only then can you stand in victory over the enemy and over life circumstances.

Hear the Truth

The Voices We Hear

There are four types of "voices" we hear speaking to us, and it is important that we learn to distinguish each one so that we are able to discern the true voice of God:

1. Your voice. In addition to your speaking voice, you also talk to yourself inside your head. You see images and pictures inside your head; you have emotions and feelings and desires. Your mind tells you what you think, your will tells you what you want, and your emotions tell you how you feel. The Bible refers to our minds, wills, and emotions as our "flesh nature."

2. Other people. People can refer to individuals or to society in general. Through conversations and advertisements, people speak to you. They tell you what you should think and how you should feel. Sometimes people say things which are true, noble, and good, and sometimes people say things which are just the opposite.

3. The devil. What he does is use spiritual influence. He puts thoughts into our minds, such as depression or a desire to sin against God, and he speaks to us through the worldly ideas and viewpoints that he has injected into other people.

4. God. This voice is the most important, but it is also the most subtle. God does not speak to us in our minds. Instead, He speaks to us in our spirits by speaking through other people, through His word, through prophecy, through dreams or visions, through a still small voice, and through our conscience.

The Voice of God

It is necessary for us as children of God to know the voice of our Father. Jesus said, "My sheep hear My voice, and I know them, and they follow Me. And I give them eternal life, and they shall never perish; neither shall anyone snatch them out of My hand" (John 10:27-28 NKJV).

When we don't know the voice of God, it is impossible to us to walk in power and authority.

Jesus' disciples had the Way in from of them all the time, but did not recognize it. We are called to do greater works than what Jesus did, but if we do not recognize the Spirit of God that lives in us, we will never fulfill our purpose. However, Jesus promises us that when we listen to His voice, we will have His life as well as His protection.

The Bible tells us that we need to be led by the Holy Spirit (see Romans 8:12-14 and Galatians 5:16-25). Therefore, it must be possible for every one of us to discern the promptings and guidance of the Holy Spirit within us. So, how do you distinguish the voice of God from all the other voices clamoring for attention?

Hearing from God is not a science. God speaks to us all the time; unfortunately, we are not listening. In order to hear God's voice and to discern His leading for your daily life, there is one key point that you need to be aware of. If you can grab hold of this one key point then you'll be hearing from God in no time. Here it is: Don't expect God to speak to you in a supernatural way!

You see, we have a natural tendency to want God to speak out loud to us in some obvious way so that we know that it was Him and so that we know what we are supposed to do. God occasionally does speak to people in an audible voice or in some other sensational way, but those are not His usual ways of speaking to us. More often, God speaks to us through the Bible, through a Christian teacher or counselor, through our life circumstances, or through the still, small voice of the Holy Spirit prompting us in a certain direction.

In his book, *How to Listen to God*[35], Charles Stanley points out four guidelines for determining the voice of God. First, God's voice is consistent with His word. Many times we ask God to give us signs when He has given us His word. This means there are certain things that you don't need to ask God about because He has already addressed those questions and concerns in His word – and God will never go against His word. So, if your mind or your heart is telling you to do something contrary to the word of God, then that is not God speaking to you.

Second, God's voice often conflicts with human wisdom. When we are busy analyzing things in our minds and trying to figure out the solutions to our problems and so on, it hinders us from hearing the Lord clearly. Now, obviously we need to use our minds and reasoning abilities throughout the day in order to do many of the things that we need to do, but the problem is that we tend to use our reasoning abilities almost exclusively and never bother to consult God on any of the decisions that we make The Bible says in Proverbs 3:5-6 (Amplified), "Lean on, trust in, and be confident in the Lord with all your heart and mind and do not rely on your own insight or understanding. In all your ways know, recognize, and acknowledge Him, and He will direct and make straight and plain your paths."

Third, God's voice clashes with a fleshly nature. To hear God, it is important to turn off our reasoning and to put our emotions into neutral when we are listening for an answer from God. Our flesh is always going to cast its vote on what it thinks we should do, but we need to ignore all of what our flesh and emotions are saying and listen to our spirits instead. Our spirits will always tell us to do the opposite of what our flesh is telling us. For example, your friends might be telling you to leave your marriage, and your flesh might be telling you to leave your marriage. But that other part of you that is telling you to stay is not the pizza you had last night – it is the spirit of God telling you to stay.

We allow our emotions to draw us out of the will of God and drown out the voice of God. God is trying to prevent us from making a mistake that we will regret for the rest of our lives, but we   have to ensure that our wills and emotions are not hindering us from hearing the voice of God. The Bible says that we must deny – disown, forget, and lose sight of – ourselves and take up our cross to follow Jesus (see Luke 9:23).   Jesus is not saying that we have to look and smell like a bum and give up our earthly possessions, but we cannot allow those things to keep us from Him. The cross is a place of <u>death</u>, which means that we should daily lose sight of ourselves in order to hear and obey God. Our desire to please Him should be greater than our desire to please ourselves.

Finally, God's voice challenges your faith. As Charles Stanley says, "God will never tell us to do anything or think of anything that sets us back spiritually. His voice leads us not into timid discipleship but into bold witness." God will always ask you to do the thing that is most likely going to grow your faith.

In addition to these truths, Stanley also points out four hindrances to hearing:

1. A false view of God
2. A closed mind (unbelief)
3. A poor self-image
4. A sinful life

Any of these things can block God's truth from reaching your heart – and that means blocking your ability to use your spiritual authority.

Speak the Truth

Sheila Walsh[36] says that "to be able to tell the truth means to have made peace with the truth." This is an important point in our search for God's truth. Yes, we need to hear God's truth by distinguishing His voice from all of the other voices, but we also need to speak His truth over our own lives and over the lives of people we encounter.

Speak the Truth to Yourself

As we already discussed, God's word has great power. He created the entire universe out of nothing just by speaking it into existence. Genesis 1:26 says that we are made in the image of God. This is not referring to the physical appearance of man only, but also according to the spirit and character of God. We were created with the ability to create, just by the words we release out of our mouth. Have you ever released a word from your mouth and a week later you saw the same thing you had spoken? That is because of the nature of God living inside of us. Because we were created in His image and according to His likeness, we are able to release words from our mouth and create our conditions.

Proverbs 18:21 says, "Death and life are in the power of the tongue, and they who indulge in it shall eat the fruit of it for death or life." The word INDULGE in the Webster dictionary means "yield to; gratifying." Whatever we yield to is what we will receive. We have the ability to change situations just by changing what comes out of our mouths.

When I first got married, my husband and I had a great many disagreements and I would deal with the matter according to the flesh. I got to a place where I was ready to leave the marriage, but I heard the Spirit of God speak to me. He began to teach me about the power of my words and that I create my conditions. He said, "Change what you are sowing, and you will change what you are receiving." Our words are seeds: whatever we plant will grow. So, I began to speak life over my husband while he was sleeping. I would lie at his feet and speak to his destiny in God; I began to declare the decree that our marriage is strong, healthy and vibrant. I also began to speak into my own life: that I am a woman of God who has purpose and a destiny that shall come to pass with my husband. I would anoint his toothbrush and declare that his words are anointed words, and when he spoke to me it would be with anointed words. I anointed his pillow and began to declare that we shall rest in peace; we shall not go to bed angry. The change did not come over night, but it did come. I spoke it just as God did in Genesis, and I saw what I spoke.

The Spirit that hovered over the water and brought to pass everything that God released is the same Spirit that now lives in us. Words have life. They are like seeds; they grow where they are planted. You don't have to be a Christian to change your conditions because the ability to create is not just for Christians since God created all mankind in His image. Therefore we can all speak life or death.

So, we as humans have powerful words since we are made in the image of God – and God's recorded word has power to accomplish whatever God sends it to do. Therefore, it makes most sense that the most powerful truth is God's revealed word spoken from the mouth of His children. So, speak the word of God out loud until it sinks down deep into your spirit and changes your life. One of the things I have learned over the years is when my emotions and my thoughts are running all over the place, I will just open the Bible to any page and began to read out loud. I immediately begin to feel the Spirit of God speaking to me. Why? Because I stopped all the confusion that my flesh was feeding me and filled my life with truth instead. God said that His word will not return to Him empty, so return His Word back to Him out of your mouth and believe that it will accomplish what He sent it to accomplish.

Speak the Truth to Others
You may be asking, "What does this have to do with spiritual authority?" I am glad you did. We cannot walk in the power of God if we are not speaking the truth. The Bible says in Ephesians 4:15 (NKJV), "But, speaking the truth in love, may grow up in all things into Him who is the head, Christ." The ability to speak the truth to others is a sign of a growing Christian, one who is becoming more like Christ. We as Christians fail to speak the truth

because we choose to spare the feelings of other people. But, we fail to realize that when we are not telling the truth we cause that person to walk blindly.

One common problem among believers is only telling part of the truth. The Apostle Paul said, "For I have not shunned to declare to you the whole counsel of God" (Acts 20:27 NKJV). Paul appreciated the truth to the point of allowing it to make those whom he loved his enemies. I see a lot of believers who tell half the story because they don't want to hurt the feelings of the other person or they don't want to deal with the hurt that will come as a result of the truth. We cannot water down the word. People often tell me that I am a hard preacher. I am not hard, but the word of God tells me that I am to preach the word, to be ready in season and out of season, to reprove, rebuke, exhort with all longsuffering and doctrine (see 2 Timothy 4:2). See, the flesh never wants what is right for the spiritual edification of a person. We must be clear and precise in our words.

Speaking the truth in love clearly exemplifies boldness. Jesus' teaching was open and plain. Jesus did not command authority by saying, "I am God, and you must obey Me." No, Jesus was able to command authority by knowing who He was, by knowing His assignment, and by remaining focused. When Jesus spoke it was with intent and purpose. He knew every word that proceeded from His mouth was truth, so it did not matter to Him if the people believed Him or not.

You should not care what people think when it comes to you obeying the word of God. Instead, you should be more afraid of disobeying God than man! But remember that speaking the truth does not mean that you don't love the person. In reality, the fact that you won't let the other person be deceived shows that you love him. The Bible says in Proverbs 27:6 (NKJV), "Faithful are the wounds of a friend, but the kisses of an enemy are deceitful." In other words, you tell the truth because you are that person's friend, because you love him.

I find that we cause more harm in people's lives when we are not honest with them. One of the greatest problems I have found in the church of America today is that we cater too much to the emotion and fleshly part of man; therefore, we would rather be deceitful and lie about simple things. Just the other day my niece came over with her mom to visit, and she had on some glasses that just did not fit. I told her mom that the glasses she had on did not look right on her and asked her why she allowed her to go out with them on. She said, "Those are her hatters, (sun hatters) and you cannot tell her anything." I disagree with that because if you're going to be a <u>diva</u> then you cannot look crazy at the same time. So we argued over whether or not to tell my niece, but then I then told my sister that I would buy her some new glasses that are right for her.

I know you're thinking that my niece is young and the mother was trying to spare her feelings, but my niece looks up to me. When she has something in her life that I do not find is a fit for her, she listens because time has proven that I will never lead her astray. She knows that I am telling her, "Baby, you are better than that. What you have is good but not good enough for you." Then I show her a more excellent way. Maybe it was just a pair of glasses, but I can't be honest with her over a fashion choice, then how can I ever hope to impact her when it comes to something more important?

Speak the word that the Lord has given to you. It is an honor to have the Lord release a word into your hearing and place you in a position to deliver that word to someone else. This can only happen from a person who transcends beyond the norm. The truth of God's word must be seen in the workings of our lives and in the words we proclaim. Spiritual authority comes when we can share with others that which the Lord God has entrusted to us.

> *"And they overcame the devil by the blood of the Lamb and by the word of their testimony, and they did not love their lives to the death" (Revelation 12:11 NKJV).*

KEYS TO USING YOUR AUTHORITY

The boy Samuel ministered before the LORD under Eli. In those days the word of the LORD was rare; there were not many visions. One night Eli, whose eyes were becoming so weak that he could barely see, was lying down in his usual place. The lamp of God had not yet gone out, and Samuel was lying down in the temple of the LORD, where the ark of God was. Then the LORD called Samuel.

Samuel answered, "Here I am." And he ran to Eli and said, "Here I am; you called me."

But Eli said, "I did not call; go back and lie down." So he went and lay down.

Again the LORD called, "Samuel!" And Samuel got up and went to Eli and said, "Here I am; you called me."

"My son," Eli said, "I did not call; go back and lie down."

Now Samuel did not yet know the LORD : The word of the LORD had not yet been revealed to him. The LORD called Samuel a third time, and Samuel got up and went to Eli and said, "Here I am; you called me."

Then Eli realized that the LORD was calling the boy. So Eli told Samuel, "Go and lie down, and if he calls you, say, 'Speak, LORD, for your servant is listening.' " So Samuel went and lay down in his place.

> *The LORD came and stood there, calling as at the other times,*
> *"Samuel! Samuel!"*
> *Then Samuel said, "Speak, for your servant is listening."*
>
> *1 Samuel 3:1-10 (NIV)*

Samuel was being trained on how to hear the voice of God, how to answer the call and how to respond when He was called. Samuel did not know God, but he knew of God. He was put in a position where he could be taught on how to hear God's call. God spoke to Samuel, but he was not listening to God's voice because it was unfamiliar to him. Once Samuel learned to recognize God's voice and God's truth, then God could use him. God spoke truth in Samuel so that Samuel could speak truth to the people of Israel. God changed Samuel's life – but he also used Samuel to change an entire nation.

IT'S YOUR TURN!

1. Which voice is easiest for you to hear?

_____
_____
_____
_____
_____

2. What steps can you take to hear God's voice more clearly?

_____
_____
_____
_____
_____

3. Do have a hard time speaking the truth in love? Why or why not? Why is it important to speak the truth to others?

_____
_____
_____
_____
_____
_____

Chapter 12: Pray in God's Spirit

Ephesians 6:10-18 (NKJV) says:

Finally, my brethren, be strong in the Lord and in the power of His might. Put on the whole armor of God, that you may be able to stand against the wiles of the devil. For we do not wrestle against flesh and blood, but against principalities, against powers, against the rulers of the darkness of this age, against spiritual hosts of wickedness in the heavenly places. Therefore take up the whole armor of God, that you may be able to withstand in the evil day, and having done all, to stand. Stand therefore, having girded your waist with truth, having put on the breastplate of righteousness, and having shod your feet with the preparation of the gospel of peace; above all, taking the shield of faith with which you will be able to quench all the fiery darts of the wicked one. And take the helmet of salvation, and the sword of the Spirit, which is the word of God; praying always with all prayer and supplication in the Spirit, being watchful to this end with all perseverance and supplication for all the saints.

Though it is mentioned among the items that make up the armor of God, prayer is often left off the list. For whatever reason, we feel the need to fight diligently on our own before possibly bringing God into the situation. This is a sad reality for us, though, because it means we often fight battles that we do not need to fight at all – simply because we want to prove ourselves.

God says that one weapon in our artillery against Satan is praying in the Spirit. Praying is simply talking to God. Praying in the Spirit means talking to God according to His word and His promises. The Bible says that we should make our prayers to God in the name of Jesus, and He will hear us. The word MAKE means "to compose, construct or design." We are to pray in such a way that our prayers are composed, constructed and designed according to the Word of God.

When Jesus' disciples asked Him to teach them how to pray, He gave them these words as a model prayer:

> *Our Father in heaven, hallowed by Your name. Your kingdom come. Your will be done on earth as it is in heaven. Give us this day our daily bread, and forgive us our debts as we forgive our debtors. And lead us not into temptation, but deliver us from the evil one. For Yours is the kingdom and the power and the glory forever. Amen (Matthew 6:9-13 NKJV).*

This model prayer will help us see the right position, the right posture, and the right perspective for our prayers.

The Right Position

Most people have misconceptions about the right prayer position. Being in the right prayer position is not about your physical location. Regardless of where your body is when you bring your needs before God, your spirit needs to be in the right place. Having the right prayer position means praying to the Father through the Son. Jesus does this in the opening line of His prayer: "Our Father in heaven."

Prayer starts by involves recognizing that God is the Father, and that He wants to give good gifts to His children (see James 1:17). This is an important point because a father is not required to give anything to someone who is not his child, but he is obligated to provide for and protect his child. While a man might choose to be a father figure for a child who is not his, he is not under any obligation or requirement to do that. If you are a Christian, then God is your Father. He has chosen to obligate Himself to you. There is no need too small or insignificant. If it matters to you, then it must matter to Him because He is a good Father. In fact, Hebrews 4:16 tells us that we can come boldly before His throne to find grace, mercy, and help.

An effective prayer life starts by praying from the position of a child approaching his father, but we must also remember that we come to the Father through the Son. Hebrews 7:25 says that Jesus lives to make intercession for us. Jesus' life, death, and resurrection make it possible for us to have access to the Father. Without Him, we would not be able to have a relationship with God, we would not be able to talk openly to God and bring Him our needs and desires. For that reason, the Bible tells us repeatedly that we should make our requests in His name.

> *And whatever you ask in My name, that I will do, that the Father may be glorified in the Son. If you ask anything in My name, I will do it (John 14:13-14 NKJV).*

> *Most assuredly, I say to you, whatever you ask the Father in My name He will give you. Until now you have asked nothing in My name. Ask, and you will receive, that your joy may be full (John 16:23-24 NKJV).*

The Right Posture

Many people believe that the right posture for prayer involves having a bowed head, folded hands, and possibly bent knees. While that is one physical posture that you can take in order to talk to God, that is not the posture that God is most concerned about. God cares more about what shape your heart is in than what shape your body is making while you talk to Him.

Our Father in heaven, hallowed be Your name . . .

Having the right prayer posture means being in a posture of humility. It starts by acknowledging that God is God and that He alone is holy. Right before giving His disciples His model prayer, Jesus told them, "When you pray, do not be like the hypocrites. For they love to pray standing in the synagogues and on the corners of the streets, that they may be seen by men . . . But when you pray, go into your room, and when you have shut your door, pray to the Father who is in the secret place" (Matthew 6:5-6 NKJV). Jesus is not saying that it is wrong to pray in church or in the streets. He is not saying that you should only pray alone and behind a closed door. Jesus is simply telling us to pray with an attitude of humility, an attitude that recognizes that we do not deserve to approach God, but we are free to because of the sacrifice of Jesus.

Give us this day our daily bread . . .

Having the right prayer posture also means coming to God through faith. The ancient Jews thought of bread as a special gift from God because of the manna He gave them in the wilderness. The manna would arrive every morning, and the people could gather what they needed for that day – but no more. They had to trust that God would provide for their needs again the next day. Jesus told us that we should have the same mindset when we bring our needs to God. We need to come to Him with faith that He will meet our needs, that He will come through in our circumstances, and that He controls every situation. In fact, Jesus promised us in Matthew 21:22 (NKJV): "Whatever you ask in My name, believing, you will receive." Having the right prayer posture means being unmoved, able, and sure-footed. While your body might be kneeling, your spirit should be standing firmly and confidently on the promises of God.

Forgive us our debts as we forgive our debtors . . .

God also expects us to pray from a posture of righteousness. Righteousness is one of those confusing religious words, but it basically means being right with God. When we approach God, we need to acknowledge and confess any sin in our lives so that nothing stands in the way of God hearing us and working on our behalf.

> *The Lord is far from the wicked, but He hears the prayer of the righteous (Proverbs 15:29 NKJV).*

In addition to receiving forgiveness for any sins we have committed, we also need to give forgiveness to anyone who has wronged us. God promises to forgive us to the same degree that we forgive others. And Jesus commands, "Whenever you stand praying, if you have anything against anyone, forgive him, that your Father in heaven may also forgive you your trespasses (Mark 11:25 NKJV).

Finally, the last part of being in the right prayer posture is being constant. Prayer is not a one-time event. Instead, God created it to be daily and continual. Effective prayer is fervent prayer. The apostle Paul encouraged us to "continue steadfastly in prayer" (Romans 12:12 NKJV), to "continue earnestly in prayer" (Colossians 4:2 NKJV), and to "pray without ceasing" (1 Thessalonians 5:17 NKJV). The words STEADFASTLY in Romans 12 and EARNESTLY in Colossians 4 is the same Greek word: PROSKARTEREO[37]. It means "to adhere to, to give unremitting care to, to persevere and not faint." That is the attitude that we should have in presenting our needs to God: I will stick to this request until I have an answer.

The Right Perspective

When we pray from the right position and the right posture, we also pray from the right perspective. The right perspective is having your mind in a place of acknowledgement and acceptance: acknowledging that God is God and accepting His will as best. As Jesus said in His model prayer, the right perspective asks for God's will to be done "on earth as it is in heaven." When we are praying with the right motives and mindset, we are really just asking God to release on earth what He has already planned and set in motion in the heavenly realm.

Prayers that come from the right perspective are prayers that God has promised to answer.

> *And this is the confidence (the assurance, the privilege of boldness) which we have in Him: we are sure that if we ask anything (make any request) according to His will (in agreement with His own plan), He listens to and hears us (1 John 5:14 Amplified).*

So, what happens when you don't know what the right thing to ask for is – when you just don't know what to pray? Even when you might not know what God's will is in a particular situation, you can just ask Him to perform His perfect plan with the confidence that He knows what it is and He will do it. When you are so confused or emotional that you simply cannot determine what to pray for, the Spirit Himself will pray for you.

> *In the same way, the Spirit helps us in our weakness. We do not know what we ought to pray for, but the Spirit himself intercedes for us with groans that words cannot express. And he who searches our hearts knows the mind of the Spirit, because the Spirit intercedes for the saints in accordance with God's will (Romans 8:26-27 NIV).*

When all else fails, pray the word, since the word of God is always in accordance with His will. The power of the spoken word of God that you release from your mouth will enforce change in the earthly realm. Instead of praying the problem, pray the promise. Instead of praying the worries, pray the word!

KEYS TO USING YOUR AUTHORITY

Remember as a child when your parents threw you into the pool and told you to swim or die? Well, in the spirit realm we must use our authority or die. To win, you must pray your way through an issue or situation. The only other alternative is to give up and give in to the problem. However, the prayer must be made in the Spirit in order to be effective. So, pray from the correct position, in the correct posture, and from the correct perspective. Pray in the confidence that your Father hears you and will answer you. Pray knowing that Jesus is making intercession for you – that He is praying for your situation, too. Finally, pray even when you don't know what to pray because the Spirit will translate your desires into the Father's desires.

IT'S YOUR TURN!

1. Do you typically take your needs and concerns to God immediately or do you try to find a solution on your own before seeking Him?

   _____

   _____

   _____

   _____

2. Is it easy or difficult for you to pray to God as your Father? Do you see Him as someone who genuinely cares about your needs or do you feel like you are bothering Him?

   _____

   _____

   _____

   _____

3. How does it make you feel to know that Jesus is praying for you?

_____

_____

_____

_____

4. Have you ever been in a situation where the Spirit needed to translate your thoughts and desires?

_____

_____

_____

_____

Chapter 13: Submit to God's Ways

My son is 17 years old. He has a license to drive during a certain time of the day until he turns 18. He has access to a car. Though he has the license and the car, he is not mature enough to drive on his own. Though he has the license and the car, he needs to grow and mature before we will allow him to have full freedom without bringing harm or danger to himself or others. He must be guided and directed. He must have someone who has full authority in the car with him while driving.

The same idea applies in a spiritual sense as well. We all have a certain degree of spiritual authority as children of God that we did not have when we were unbelievers. But, God cannot trust us fully to exercise our authority until we begin to grow and to demonstrate spiritual maturity. If God gives us complete freedom of authority with His power and spiritual gifts before we are mature enough to handle them then we might end up hurting ourselves or others.

I received Jesus as my Lord and Savior at the age of 17. I was so excited about being saved that I wanted to do everything for the Lord and possess the power that came along with it. What I did not understand was that I was young in the Lord and very immature. Therefore, I did not have the wisdom to complete the task. I was so eager to embark upon my desire, but I did not possess the knowledge and wisdom to complete it.

The apostle Paul said that an heir owns the whole estate, but the heir cannot walk in the fullness of his authority until he grows up (see Galatians 4:1-7). When we receive salvation we become God's children, meaning that we are heirs of God and co-heirs with Christ (see Romans 8:15-17). We start off as spiritual infants (see 1 Corinthians 3:1), and we must begin cooperating with the sanctifying work of the Holy Spirit so that we grow up and become mature in Christ (see Ephesians 4:11-16). It is only as we "come up higher" in spiritual maturity that God will be able to trust us with greater levels of spiritual authority.

One of the things I have learned in my walk with God is that maturity grows through obedience in God. It is so easy and natural for us to do what we want to do instead of being obedient to God, but we cannot live worldly lives and then expect God's power to be available to us when we feel like using it.

When I met my husband, I wanted to leave my church and attend church with him. I went to my pastor at the time and explained to him what I was feeling, and he told me it was not the time to leave. That is something I did not want to hear. I knew this was my husband, and I was not taking no for an answer. Weeks went by before I called my pastor on the phone and told him that I was leaving the church so that I could attend church with my fiancé. He did not agree with my decision at the time, but being the man of God that he is, he released me. Years later, after I became a pastor myself, the Lord began to deal with me about leaving the church the way I did. The Lord showed me that my pastor saw that God was still working on me. He was not saying that Darrylle was not my husband, but that there was something in me that was not ready for marriage at that time. I needed to mature and grow up. I said, "Lord, why did You take four years before you brought this to my attention?" He said, "Because you were not mature enough to handle this level of rebuke until now."

A mature Christian is one who is led by the Spirit. The Bible says in Galatians 5:16 that we are to walk and live habitually in the Spirit. In other words, the Spirit of the living God should guide and direct our every step. Being led by God must be a part of our daily lives. We have to bring our will, emotions, and thoughts under complete submission to the Spirit of God. When we are led by the Spirit, we will not fulfill the lust of the flesh and its desires. According to Colossians 3:5, we must put our human natures to death. Human nature is the emotions and thoughts that lead to sexual immorality, impurity, lust, evil desires, greed, and idolatry. We have control over these things. We have the power to stop if we choose, but we do not choose to stop because we like our sin. We enjoy the way it makes us feel and the excitement it brings.

However, when we are in Christ we are a new creation. All old things pass away and all things become new (see 2 Corinthians 5:17). As long as we are walking according to the flesh, we cannot walk in obedience to God. We are still submitted to the old man. True authority and power come when we can control our flesh and ungodly desires. We must take off everything that is natural or human and put on the Spirit of God.

KEYS TO USING YOUR AUTHORITY

Paul painted a picture of a mature Christian in Philippians 3. He said that those of us who are spiritually mature should think this way:

> *Those things were important to me, but now I think they are worth nothing because of Christ. Not only those things, but I think that all things are worth nothing compared with the greatness of knowing Christ Jesus my Lord. Because of him, I*

have lost all those things, and now I know they are worthless trash. This allows me to have Christ and to belong to him. Now I am right with God, not because I followed the law, but because I believed in Christ. God uses my faith to make me right with him. I want to know Christ and the power that raised him from the dead. I want to share in his sufferings and become like him in his death. Then I have hope that I myself will be raised from the dead.

I do not mean that I am already as God wants me to be. I have not yet reached that goal, but I continue trying to reach it and to make it mine. Christ wants me to do that, which is the reason he made me his. Brothers and sisters, I know that I have not yet reached that goal, but there is one thing I always do. Forgetting the past and straining toward what is ahead, I keep trying to reach the goal and get the prize for which God called me through Christ to the life above (Philippians 3:7-14 NCV).

The life of a Christian is an ever-growing, ever-changing, ever-learning life. Paul said it is a journey where we keep pressing forward until the day God takes us home. And on the way, we should become more and more like Christ.

However, Paul also said that God will show us areas where we need improvement.

And if there are things you do not agree with, God will make them clear to you. But we should continue following the truth we already have (Philippians 3:15-16 NCV).

If you are honestly and earnestly seeking God's ways, He will show you where you need to change. But, only if you are walking in the truth you already have. If you are stubbornly refusing to obey God in the areas He has already revealed to you, why would He show you other things? However, He promises that He will not let you miss anything if you are growing up in His image.

IT'S YOUR TURN!

1. What are some "old nature" things that you need to take off?

_____

_____

_____

_____

2. What are some "new nature" things that we need to put on?

    _____

    _____

    _____

    _____

3. Is your Christian life one that is growing and changing, or have you become stagnant? Regardless of where you are, where might God be leading you from here?

    _____

    _____

    _____

    _____

    _____

    _____

    _____

    _____

    _____

Chapter 14: Stand in God's Victory

When we depend upon God and not ourselves, that Bible says that we can do all things through Christ who gives us strength (see Philippians 4:13). You have to follow Biblical precepts – the steps outlined in this book - but when you have done all you can do, then stand firm. You have authority, and you live in Jesus' victory.

Remember when Jesus was in the desert being tempted by the devil? He didn't shout at the devil. He didn't call up His lawyer. He didn't try to prove who He was with a lot of gimmicks and threats. He used His authority simply, quietly, and completely confident that Satan would submit to authority of the Son of God. Jesus was completely confident because he was in the will of the Father.

You have the same confidence, the same authority. Satan knows this. You don't have to argue with the devil. You do not need to discuss or question. You are a blood-bought child of the living God. Learn Satan's tactics and know God's word. Stay in a state of prayer and grow in your Christian maturity. Then stand in the confidence of knowing that Satan must submit to your authority. Trust God to fight for you.

So, how do you stand in God's victory?

Arm yourself.

> Put on the full armor of God so that you can take your stand
> against the devil's schemes (Ephesians 6:11 NIV).

Do not be afraid.

> This is what the LORD says to you: "Do not be afraid or
> discouraged because of this vast army, for the battle is not
> yours, but God's. You will not have to fight this battle. Take
> up your positions; stand firm and see the deliverance the Lord
> will give you. Do not be afraid; do not be discouraged. Go
> out to face them tomorrow, and the Lord will be with you" (2
> Chronicles 20:15b, 17 NIV).

Stand firm.

> *Resist the devil and he will flee from you (James 4:7 NKJV).*

It is not my personality, my good looks, my past or the clothes I wear. It is the authority of the Lord Jesus Christ who died on Calvary and was raised from the dead and will come again in the flesh to walk this earth. You can stand firm on His promises.

IT'S YOUR TURN!

1. What do you depend on instead of depending on Jesus?

   _____

   _____

   _____

   _____

   _____

2. How would your life be different if you stood in the victory you already have instead of living in fear?

   _____

   _____

   _____

   _____

   _____

About the Author

Here is a voice of the 21st century. A voice for the voiceless, one who dares to stand up boldly to declare a message of hope, and truth – compelling the attention of those who seek to discover their purpose in life and launch into their destiny.

Angela Hood is the co-founder along with her husband Bishop D.G. Hood of New Life Worship Center Ministries International in Hollywood, Florida. She is also a Life Coach, Motivational Speaker, Pastor, Preacher, Teacher, Wife and Mother. Angela has dedicated her life to pulling others out of their circumstances so that they can focus in on God's unique plan of destiny for their lives. Pastor Angela Hoods Ministry focuses on empowering believers in the Kingdom of God. She preaches real life messages that are life changing.

Angela's current business websites:

www.ardysslife.com/angelahood – Women's Intimate Apparel

www.nlwcmi.org – New Life Worship Center Miniseries International

www.angelahood.com – Angela Hood Ministries

Chapter 1

1   "authority." Dictionary.com Unabridged (v 1.1). Random House, Inc. 04 May. 2009. <Dictionary.com http://dictionary1.classic.reference.com/browse/authority>.

2   Blue Letter Bible. "Dictionary and Word Search for apostolos (Strong's 652)". Blue Letter Bible. 1996-2009. 4 May 2009. <http://www.blueletterbible.org/lang/lexicon/lexicon.cfm?Strongs=G652&t=KJV>

3   Blue Letter Bible. "Dictionary and Word Search for did□mi (Strong's 1325)". Blue Letter Bible. 1996-2009. 4 May 2009. <http://www.blueletterbible.org/lang/lexicon/lexicon.cfm?Strongs=G1325&t=KJV>

4   Blue Letter Bible. "Dictionary and Word Search for dynamis (Strong's 1411)". Blue Letter Bible. 1996-2009. 4 May 2009. <http://www.blueletterbible.org/lang/lexicon/lexicon.cfm?Strongs=G1411&t=KJV>

5   Blue Letter Bible. "Dictionary and Word Search for exousia (Strong's 1849)". Blue Letter Bible. 1996-2009. 4 May 2009. <http://www.blueletterbible.org/lang/lexicon/lexicon.cfm?Strongs=G1849&t=KJV>

6   Blue Letter Bible. "Dictionary and Word Search for k□ryss□ (Strong's 2784)". Blue Letter Bible. 1996-2009. 4 May 2009. <http://www.blueletterbible.org/lang/lexicon/lexicon.cfm?Strongs=G2784&t=KJV>

Chapter 3

7   Blue Letter Bible. "Dictionary and Word Search for k□ryss□ (Strong's 2784)". Blue Letter Bible. 1996-2009. 4 May 2009. <http://www.blueletterbible.org/lang/lexicon/lexicon.cfm?Strongs=G2784&t=KJV>

8   Blue Letter Biblc. "Dictionary and Word Search for therapeu□ (Strong's 2323)". Blue Letter Bible. 1996-2009. 4 May 2009. <http://www.blueletterbible.org/lang/lexicon/lexicon.cfm?Strongs=G2323&t=KJV >

9   Blue Letter Bible. "Dictionary and Word Search for iaomai (Strong's 2390)". Blue Letter Bible. 1996-2009. 4 May 2009. <http://www.blueletterbible.org/lang/lexicon/lexicon.cfm?Strongs=G2390&t=KJV>

10 Blue Letter Bible. "Dictionary and Word Search for nosos (Strong's 3554)". Blue Letter Bible. 1996-2009. 4 May 2009. <http://www.blualetterbible. org/lang/lexicon/lexicon.cfm?Strongs=G3554&t=KJV>

11 Blue Letter Bible. "Dictionary and Word Search for asthene☐ (Strong's 770)". Blue Letter Bible. 1996-2009. 4 May 2009. <http://www. blueletterbible.org/lang/lexicon/lexicon.cfm?Strongs=G770&t=KJV>

12 Blue Letter Bible. "Dictionary and Word Search for daimonion (Strong's 1140)". Blue Letter Bible. 1996-2009. 4 May 2009. <http://www. blueletterbible.org/lang/lexicon/lexicon.cfm?Strongs=G1140&t=KJV>

13 Blue Letter Bible. "Dictionary and Word Search for de☐ (Strong's 1210)". Blue Letter Bible. 1996-2009. 4 May 2009. <http://www.blualetterbible. org/lang/lexicon/lexicon.cfm?Strongs=G1210&t=KJV>

14 Blue Letter Bible. "Dictionary and Word Search for ly☐ (Strong's 3089)". Blue Letter Bible. 1996-2009. 4 May 2009. <http://www.blualetterbible. org/lang/lexicon/lexicon.cfm?Strongs=G3089&t=KJV>

Chapter 5

15 Yancey, Philip. *Disappointment with God*. Grand Rapids: Zondervan, 1997.

16 Tenney, Tommy. *God Chasers*. Shippensburg, PA: Destiny Image, 1999.

Chapter 8

Portions of this chapter were borrowed with permission from "Before the Beginning", a chapter in *Through the Bible: Genesis*, a Bible study by Kelly Lapp.

17 Walsh, Sheila. *God Has a Dream for Your Life*. Nashville: Thomas Nelson, 2007.

18 Blue Letter Bible. "Dictionary and Word Search for ai☐nios (Strong's 166)". Blue Letter Bible. 1996-2009. 4 May 2009. <http://www.blualetterbible. org/lang/lexicon/lexicon.cfm?Strongs=G166&t=KJV>

19 Blue Letter Bible. "Dictionary and Word Search for progin☐sk☐ (Strong's 4267)". Blue Letter Bible. 1996-2009. 4 May 2009. <http://www. blueletterbible.org/lang/lexicon/lexicon.cfm?Strongs=G4267&t=KJV>

20 Blue Letter Bible. "Dictionary and Word Search for prooriz☐ (Strong's 4309)". Blue Letter Bible. 1996-2009. 4 May 2009. <http://www. blueletterbible.org/lang/lexicon/lexicon.cfm?Strongs=G4309&t=KJV>

21 Blue Letter Bible. "Dictionary and Word Search for symmorphos (Strong's 4832)". Blue Letter Bible. 1996-2009. 4 May 2009. <http://www.blueletterbible.org/lang/lexicon/lexicon.cfm?Strongs=G4832&t=KJV>

22 Blue Letter Bible. "Dictionary and Word Search for kale☐ (Strong's 2564)". Blue Letter Bible. 1996-2009. 4 May 2009. <http://www.blueletterbible.org/lang/lexicon/lexicon.cfm?Strongs=G2564&t=KJV >

23 Blue Letter Bible. "Dictionary and Word Search for dikaio☐ (Strong's 1344)". Blue Letter Bible. 1996-2009. 4 May 2009. <http://www.blueletterbible.org/lang/lexicon/lexicon.cfm?Strongs=G1344&t=KJV>

24 Blue Letter Bible. "Dictionary and Word Search for doxaz☐ (Strong's 1392)". Blue Letter Bible. 1996-2009. 4 May 2009. <http://www.blueletterbible.org/lang/lexicon/lexicon.cfm?Strongs=G1392&t=KJV>

25 Blue Letter Bible. "Dictionary and Word Search for eklegomai (Strong's 1586)". Blue Letter Bible. 1996-2009. 4 May 2009. <http://www.blueletterbible.org/lang/lexicon/lexicon.cfm?Strongs=G1586&t=KJV>

26 Blue Letter Bible. "Dictionary and Word Search for prothesis (Strong's 4286)". Blue Letter Bible. 1996-2009. 4 May 2009. <http://www.blueletterbible.org/lang/lexicon/lexicon.cfm?Strongs=G4286&t=KJV>

27 Blue Letter Bible. "Dictionary and Word Search for charis (Strong's 5485)". Blue Letter Bible. 1996-2009. 4 May 2009. <http://www.blueletterbible.org/lang/lexicon/lexicon.cfm?Strongs=G5485&t=KJV>

28 Kadlecek, Jo. *Desperate Women of the Bible*. Grand Rapids: Baker Books, 2006

Chapter 9
Portions of this chapter were borrowed with permission from "Who is Satan?", a chapter in *Teach Me the Bible: Foundations*, a Bible study by Kelly Lapp.

29 Blue Letter Bible. "Dictionary and Word Search for heylel (Strong's 1966)". Blue Letter Bible. 1996-2009. 4 May 2009. <http://www.blueletterbible.org/lang/lexicon/lexicon.cfm?Strongs=H1966&t=KJV >

30 Blue Letter Bible. "Dictionary and Word Search for topos (Strong's 5117)". Blue Letter Bible. 1996-2009. 4 May 2009. <http://www.blueletterbible.org/lang/lexicon/lexicon.cfm?Strongs=G5117&t=KJV >

Chapter 10
Portions of this chapter were borrowed with permission from "What is the Bible?", a chapter in *Teach Me the Bible: Foundations*, a Bible study by Kelly Lapp.

31 Blue Letter Bible. "Dictionary and Word Search for theopneustos (Strong's 2315)". Blue Letter Bible. 1996-2009. 4 May 2009. <http://www.blueletterbible.org/lang/lexicon/lexicon.cfm?Strongs=G2315&t=KJV>

32 Blue Letter Bible. "Dictionary and Word Search for rh⬚ma (Strong's 4487)". Blue Letter Bible. 1996-2009. 4 May 2009. <http://www.blueletterbible.org/lang/lexicon/lexicon.cfm?Strongs=G4487&t=KJV>

33 Blue Letter Bible. "Dictionary and Word Search for logos (Strong's 3056)". Blue Letter Bible. 1996-2009. 4 May 2009. <http://www.blueletterbible.org/lang/lexicon/lexicon.cfm?Strongs=G3056&t=KJV>

34 Blue Letter Bible. "Dictionary and Word Search for tsaphan (Strong's 6845)". Blue Letter Bible. 1996-2009. 4 May 2009. <http://www.blueletterbible.org/lang/lexicon/lexicon.cfm?Strongs=H6845&t=KJV >

Chapter 11
35 Stanley, Charles. *How to Listen to God*. Nashville: Thomas Nelson, 2002.

36 Walsh, Sheila. *God Has a Dream for Your Life*. Nashville: Thomas Nelson, 2007.

Chapter 12
37 Blue Letter Bible. "Dictionary and Word Search for proskartere⬚ (Strong's 4342)". Blue Letter Bible. 1996-2009. 4 May 2009. <http://www.blueletterbible.org/lang/lexicon/lexicon.cfm?Strongs=G4342&t=KJV>